In *The Good Portion – Ch*  biblical understanding
I walked away with a gre

to invest deeply in my local church for the glory of God.

Hunter Beless

Host of the Journeywomen Podcast

Author of *Read it, See it, Say it, Sing it*

Erin Wheeler has written a book that is useful for understanding and life. It is faithful and fun, biblically informed and rich in simple, direct illustrations. Would you like a book to help explain to a friend what the church is, what it's like and why it's so important? This is that book.

Mark Dever

Senior Pastor, Capitol Hill Baptist Church, Washington DC

and President, 9Marks.org

Women make up half the church and yet resources by women, for women about the church are scarce. I was delighted, then, to read Erin Wheeler's *The Good Portion: Church*. Wheeler is an engaging writer and a solid theologian whose own love for Christ's bride shines on every page. If you are a woman looking to understand God's design for the church, this book will be an invaluable resource. And even if your convictions about polity or sacraments differ from Wheeler's, you will still find plenty here to ignite your love for your own local church. This book refreshed my gratitude to Christ for redeeming and gathering His church—I trust it will do the same for you.

Megan Hill

Editor, The Gospel Coalition

Author, *A Place to Belong: Learning to Love the Local Church*

If you love Jesus, you will increasingly love what He loves. And Jesus loves the local church. Many believers, though, settle for a 'church-optional' Christianity (I once did—it's one of my biggest regrets). Such a posture can understandably be downstream from distrust—from a negative, even tragic, church experience. In a fallen world, many churches are indeed sick. But others are healthy. And in infinite wisdom and love, Jesus has designed the Christian life—your Christian life—to orbit around a healthy church. Erin Wheeler wants to show you why that's terrific news. Sister, the truths awaiting you here are not just necessary, like medicine. They are also beautiful, like the Messiah Himself.

Matt Smethurst

Pastor, River City Baptist Church, Richmond, Virginia; managing editor, The Gospel Coalition; author, *Before You Share Your Faith*, *Before You Open Your Bible,* and *Deacons*

This book helps us to see clearly that the church is at the very heart, the very center of God's eternal purposes for mankind. I thoroughly enjoyed reading it and found it enormously clear, accessible and helpful. While reading, it was obvious to me that Erin loves the local church and her passion for the church stirred up in me afresh a love for my local church. It is an excellent resource for believers around the world who want to learn more about the Doctrine of the Church and also to teach others. I most definitely intend to use this resource in my church with the women! Each chapter ends with some great discussion questions which I found to be very beneficial. Thank you, dear Erin, for explaining to us what the Church is and ehat the Church looks like!! I pray that it will be a blessing to many.

Malini Ruth Singh

Satya Vachan Church, Lucknow, India

The role of the local church is both underestimated and misunderstood in our day. What a welcome resource *The Good Portion – Church* is. It serves to clarify the vital doctrine of the church and how we as women must embrace it for all the right reasons. I so appreciate Erin Wheeler's passion coupled with her winsome style in this well researched book. How we need voices like hers to make a clarion call to women with theological truth set forth plainly!

Mary K. Mohler
Director of Seminary Wives Institute at Southern Seminary,
Louisville, Kentucky
Author of *Growing in Gratitude*

Weighty and yet practical, Erin's book is a rare find. Her passion for the church is visible and contagious. Her clear and personal writing style makes this easy to read and accessible for a new believer, while full of rich teaching for the seasoned saint. Reading this book will change the way you relate to your local church. If our churches are to be places that 'protect and proclaim His glory to the world' then they need to be filled with people who have been transformed by the truths of this book.

Adrienne Lawrence
Pastor's Wife, Charles Simeon Trust instructor, Bible teacher

A book on the value of the local church is always needed, but how much more after the last few years of stopping and starting because of a pandemic. Erin Wheeler writes as one who not only loves the church, but knows how to bring others into her love for Christ's bride. This book is well-written, scripturally sound, and a beautiful invitation to love the local church.

Courtney Reissig
Author, *Teach Me to Feel: Worshiping Through the Psalms in Every Season of Life*

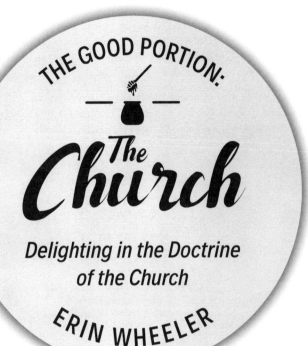

THE GOOD PORTION:

The Church

Delighting in the Doctrine of the Church

ERIN WHEELER

SERIES EDITOR: KERI FOLMAR

CHRISTIAN
FOCUS

Copyright © Erin Wheeler 2022

paperback ISBN 978-1-5271-0834-9
ebook ISBN 978-1-5271-0881-3

10 9 8 7 6 5 4 3 2 1

Published in 2022
by
Christian Focus Publications, Ltd.
Geanies House, Fearn,
Ross-shire, IV20 1TW, Scotland.
www.christianfocus.com

Cover design by Pete Barnsley

Printed and bound by
Bell & Bain, Glasgow

CONTENTS

To the saints of
Capitol Hill Baptist Church, Third Avenue Baptist Church,
and University Baptist Church.
You have shown me what it means to worship together
as we await the return of our King.

'Now to him who is able to do far more abundantly than all that we
ask or think, according to the power at work within us,
*to him be glory **in the church***
and in Christ Jesus
throughout all generations, forever and ever.
Amen' (Eph. 3:20-21).

Series Preface

The priest pleaded with the young woman to renounce her faith and embrace the Roman Catholic Church. Only sixteen years of age, Lady Jane Grey had been the Protestant Queen of England for nine short days. Her cousin, the staunch Catholic Queen Mary, would pardon her life if only she would recant. Instead, Jane resolutely walked to the scaffold and publicly declared:

> I pray you all, good Christian people, to bear me witness that
> I die a true Christian woman. I do look to be saved by no other
> means, but only by the mercy of God, in the blood of his only
> Son Jesus Christ.[1]

Jane Grey's confidence lay in the sure hope of the resurrection for
those who trust in Christ alone.

Ann Hasseltine struggled to make her decision. She loved
Adoniram and was even drawn by the excitement of exploring
foreign lands. But was she willing to give up all the comforts of
home for the dangers of the unknown? Could she endure leaving
loved ones never to meet them again in this life? Adoniram Judson
was headed to India in 1811 and had asked Ann to join him as
his wife. Never before had any woman left America to become
a missionary to unreached people. Ann's contemplation of Jesus
made the decision for her. In her diary she wrote:

> When I get near to God, and discern the excellence of the
> character of the Lord Jesus, and especially his power and
> willingness to save, I feel desirous, that the whole world should
> become acquainted with this Savior. I am not only willing to
> spend my days among the heathen, in attempting to enlighten
> and save them, but I find much pleasure in the prospect. Yes,
> I am quite willing to give up temporal comforts, and live a life
> of hardship and trial, if it be the will of God.[2]

Mary King stirred her pot as she contemplated Sunday's sermon.
'Cook' was a faithful, godly woman who not only prepared hearty
meals for the boys at Newmarket School, but also served up 'good
strong Calvinistic doctrine' to fifteen-year-old Charles Spurgeon,
who credited her with teaching him his theology:

---

1   Quoted in Faith Cook, *Lady Jane Grey: Nine Day Queen of England*
     (Darlington: Evangelical Press, 2004), p. 198.

2   Quoted in Sharon James, *My Heart in His Hands* (Durham: Evangelical
     Press, 1998), p. 38.

Many a time we have gone over the covenant of grace together, and talked of the personal election of the saints, their union to Christ, their final perseverance, and what vital godliness meant; and I do believe that I learnt more from her than I should have learned from any six doctors of divinity of the sort we have nowadays.[3]

Cook dished out spiritual food as well as meat and potatoes, and Charles Spurgeon never forgot what she taught him.

A queen, a bride and a cook: they were all steeped in Christian doctrine – biblical teaching about God. These women didn't just endure theology. They relished the truths of the Christian faith. Doctrine affected their lives and overflowed to impact others.

As women in the modern world we lead busy lives. We may juggle the responsibilities of work and school and home. We wake up in the morning to dirty laundry and an inbox full of email. We go to bed at night after washing dishes, chasing deadlines and rocking babies to sleep. Sometimes life is overwhelming and sometimes it is just mundane. The God who sent His Son into the world to rescue sinners gives meaning to both the overwhelming and the mundane. He created us to enjoy knowing Him, and it is in knowing Him that we find both meaning and joy. Psalm 16:11 says, 'You make known to me the path of life; in your presence there is fullness of joy; at your right hand are pleasures forevermore.' This is why Jesus commended Mary 'who sat at the Lord's feet and listened to his teaching' (Luke 10:39). In the midst of a busy household, Mary was enjoying doctrine – Jesus' teaching about Himself and His Father. She chose 'the good portion' and couldn't tear herself away.

How do you feel about doctrine? Do you dwell on the gospel, meditate on the excellencies of Christ and discuss the doctrines of grace? Do you relish the truths of the Christian faith? This series of books on doctrine for women is an attempt to fuel your enjoyment

---

3   C.H. Spurgeon, *Autobiography:Volume 1 The Early Years* (Edinburgh: Banner of Truth Trust, 1962), p. 39.

of God by encouraging a greater knowledge of Him. It is our hope that the biblical doctrines laid out here will not only increase your head-knowledge but will be driven down into your heart, bearing fruit in your life and overflowing into the lives of others.

Keri Folmar
September 2016

Introduction:

It Doesn't Matter Until it Does

Why study the church?

It feels like it doesn't matter...until it does.

'Why? Why does anybody need to know anything about my life at all? What I do with my life is my business, not the church's!' And so it came. A torrent of anger, confusion and frustration that this thing called 'church' would dare to intrude upon the private affairs of her members.

The discipling date with my friend took a turn that day I didn't see coming. In the members' meeting the night before, the elders of our church expressed concern for two members undergoing a difficult time in their marriage, and in consultation with the couple, asked the congregation to pray for them. As spiritual family, they wanted us to be aware so that we might pray and care well for these struggling members.

But my friend couldn't hear the care and concern. All she could hear was judgment.

They need to leave them alone and not flaunt their private information around for everyone to ogle over and judge. 'People don't actually pray for one another in the church. They judge them!' Her words were barbed, but her eyes were begging for answers. Sadly, my answers were not ones she wanted to hear.

Her anger was fed not only by her confusion, but also her past church experiences. She had seen 'prayer requests' used as a means of gossip, where the phrase, 'I'll pray for you,' actually meant, 'Don't worry, I'll be sure to spread that news about you around town under the guise of "prayer."' Instead of being loved by others, she had been gossiped about by others. Her church experience had been one of abuse and not care. I fear she's not alone.

Why the doctrine of the church matters

My husband is the lead pastor of a church and a committed expositional preacher (*expositional* means that the point of the sermon is the point of the text applied to the hearts of the people). Recently, he veered from his norm in order to preach a topical series entitled, 'What Does it Mean to be Baptist?' Sounds like a real show-stopper, huh? There were many important truths in those sermons surrounding the doctrine of the church, but it was one line that resonated with me as I sat across the table from this friend: 'These doctrines won't seem to matter until they do.' Sitting there with her, I realized how right he was. At that moment, the doctrine of the church mattered to me and my friend! The only way through the confusion was to look at God's prescriptions for His people. His Word has everything we need for life and godliness (2 Pet. 1:3), and this includes how we 'do' church. 'The doctrine of the church is of the utmost importance. It is the most visible part of Christian theology, and it is vitally connected with every other part.'[1]

At the root of the struggle wasn't the elders' 'crazy' and 'obnoxious' ideas of how to 'do church,' but rather a misunderstanding of what the church is and why it exists in the first place. My friend lacked a grasp on the gospel and how that gospel is made public through the witness of God's people. She desperately needed to understand why a local body of believers should unite themselves in this dark world as a beacon of light and a witness to the watching world. At the end of the day, she wanted to relate to God on her own terms, and she couldn't see how, in the church, we're actually called to relate to Him and His people on His terms.

A shot of spiritual Red Bull?

Unfortunately, the situation I faced with my friend isn't unusual. For some, the biblical understanding of church is seen as a crutch. For others, this kind of commitment looks more like a cult. In an age of individualism and consumerism, church often morphs into 'Which service fits my schedule this week?' or 'Give me Jesus, but not His people.' Living in the South, I hear people say, 'I grew up here. It's just what we do. It's what we've always done.' Church becomes an event we attend or a place we occasionally visit, not a people to whom we belong.

When you think about church what comes to your mind? Do you choose a church based on what's convenient for you? What works with your schedule or for your children's activities? Maybe you decide based on whether the style is a 'fit' for you. Take a moment and consider, why do you bother to go to church? What

---

1   Mark Dever, *The Church* (Nashville, TN: B&H Publishing, 2012), p. ix

things bring you back each week? Is it simply for what you can get out of it? A weekly shot of spiritual Red Bull?

Generally speaking, evangelicals don't think much about the church. We tend to categorize theological issues into two camps: *essential for salvation* and *unimportant*. The church often gets lumped into that large bucket of things that may be good, but are more optional than essential. The church may not be necessary for salvation, but is it wise to classify it as unimportant? One Christian comedian even jested recently that it's just a matter of time before virtual reality churches become a viable option for Christians, giving people the choice of what kind of service they feel like streaming into their homes on any given day at any time of day. We may giggle a bit inwardly at this idea, but we're already there! The question before us is, would that really be a bad thing?

The worldwide Covid-19 pandemic propelled these questions, hovering nebulously over our heads, to the forefront of our lives. What is church? What is it for? Who is it for? What is to be done there? Does God give us instructions in His Word, or are we left to our own creativity and ingenuity? Is it really God's idea, or simply a man-made experiment?

My deepest desire in writing this book is that you come away realizing God has very clear things to say in His Word about His church that should not be disregarded. God's Word shows us the doctrine of the church is of vital importance. The Bible visibly displays and intricately connects every part of Christian theology. The famous twentieth-century Welsh preacher Dr. Martin Lloyd Jones noted that, 'the church is not a place where people are to be entertained, or where people come to sit and listen either to singing or to the accounts of other people's experiences, coupled with a brief, light, comfortable message.' He continued, 'If we are to become grown men (and I assume he means women here too), if we are to rise to the height of our 'high calling in Christ Jesus', and to be virile Christians in this tragic modern world, then we must face these great and glorious doctrines, and so exercise our minds, our understanding, and all our sense, that we begin to have some dim conception of ourselves in this great setting and context of the body of Christ.'[2]

I'm not sure why you picked up this book. Maybe you've never been a part of a church and are wondering what it's all about. Maybe you're a skeptic and cynic. Or maybe you've been hurt by poor church experiences. My prayer is that you find answers here, but even more that you find the true hope that can only be found in the Lord and Savior, Jesus Christ.

Some readers may come from a more traditional church background but struggle to articulate why they hold to their ideas of church beyond a simple, 'That's how I was raised,' or, 'That's how we've always done it.' Read on sister. In a world where contemporary culture is consuming our traditions, we need robust biblical convictions that sharpen the mind and warm the heart.

Others of you may loathe the idea of committing yourself to some kind of 'institution' or man-made construct called the church. You and Jesus are copacetic. Wherever two or three or gathered, Jesus promises to be with us, right? Why do we need to complicate or formalize it so much? You too should read on!

Use this resource for yourself or walk through it with another sister as a means of discipling them – 'encourage one another daily, as long as it is called "Today," so that none of you may be hardened by sin's deceitfulness' (Heb. 3:13, NIV). It could also be used with a group of women for a book study. There are questions at the end of each chapter, making it a useful tool for these purposes.

Moms, you may want to better know how to train your children on the importance of committing to the local church, for one day in the near future they will be leaving home. Will committing themselves to a local church be one of their priorities?

---

2   Lloyd-Jones, Dr. Martin, *God's Ultimate Purpose: An Exposition of Ephesians 1*, (Grand Rapids, MI: Baker Books, 1978) p. 424

Wherever you are today in your understanding or experience, God's church is a doctrine worth pondering and pursuing. God's Word tells us the church is the bride of Christ. And it is in the church where Christians living together in committed community make the gospel both visible and tangible.

So may this little book grow not just your knowledge of the church, but your love and affection for the gift the church is to God's people. Use this resource to better understand why the church matters and why it should matter to *you*.

It's been said that the church is the meaning of human history.[3] If so, shouldn't it be worthy of not just your attention, but your admiration, appreciation, and devotion? I pray so. It wasn't always for me. That's why I'm writing, and why I invite you to learn alongside me.

---

3   Carl Trueman, *Fools Rush In Where Monkeys Fear to Tread*, (Phillipsburg, NJ: P&R Publishing, 2011) p.116

Part One

What is the Church?

Chapter 1

A Divine Idea:
God's Plan and Purpose for the Church

The Church's one foundation
Is Jesus Christ her Lord;
She is His new creation
By water and the Word:
From heav'n He came and sought her
To be His holy Bride;
With His own blood He bought her,
And for her life He died.

'The Church's One Foundation'
S. J. Stone, 1866

Growing up with Christian parents who regularly participated in church services and activities, I lived under the false assumption that others held the same idea of 'church' as I did. But at eighteen, I headed off to a Christian college and realized my error. Following our first week of classes, my new dorm-mates and I began discussing which church we should attend on Sunday. Some questioned whether or not we needed to attend church at all. 'I can have my quiet time in the morning and we have the evening prayer service on campus Sunday nights. That's really all I need.' Though I didn't agree, I also didn't have a biblical or thoughtful response. Years later the fruit of each of their various decisions was evident in their lives.

After my husband and I married we lived together in six different states, all with their own cultural concepts around 'church.' On one of those moves, we found ourselves immersed in a culturally Christian environment. Most of my coworkers identified as believers in the Lord Jesus, but many were either disconnected or, at best, loosely connected with any church in the area. Still clinging to what seemed like some cultural kudos for claiming Christianity, they were happy to accept the Christian label without identifying with any particular church. The conversations were different from those in college, but the underlying issues were the same.

These illustrations show just some of the confusion around the idea of 'church.' Right now I find myself writing in my home in the middle of the Covid-19 pandemic. Churches around the world have been unable to gather together for months now. These new restrictions have left many asking themselves, What is church? Can't we just 'do church' online? Maybe we just have church at home with our immediate family? This pandemic has highlighted some of the confusion that already exists about the church.

God's Idea

So let's ask that question! What is 'church?' What is the point of 'going to church?' Why should I bother being a part of one today? We'll be addressing these questions in part one of this book. In answering, we'd be remiss not to look to God's Word for the answers, for it's there that we learn that *the church has been God's idea all along*.

The church is actually where we look to see what God is, and has been, doing in the world. It's even been referred to as 'a colony of heaven.'[1] This means the doctrine of the church, formally referred to as *ecclesiology*, isn't just for the professionals with seminary degrees. The doctrine of the church is for everyone! Yet theologian Ligon Duncan has sadly noted, 'Ecclesiology is indisputably one of evangelicalism's great weaknesses, in part because of subjectivism, individualism, and pragmatism.'[2] Today's worldviews permeate much of our thinking, shouting (or sometimes quietly whispering): 'There is no absolute truth;' 'Every person has their own truth;' Nothing good comes from spending your time at church;' 'Churches are all corrupt.' Much more time, effort, money, energy, and study have been put into finding the 'secret sauce' to make a church 'work' than in looking at what God's Word tells us about His creation, His divine idea, the church. It's imperative as believers in the Lord Jesus Christ that we better know and understand the picture, gift, and responsibility He has given us in and through His church. How else will you be able to answer the question, 'Why do you go to church?'? Do you know why?

If the church is God's idea, then He has a plan for it and a purpose. To help us identify this, we will walk through the timeline of biblical history, looking at this reality manifested on the pages of Scripture. We'll also see how that plan involves a universal and local church as well as an invisible and visible church. We will close by looking at God's purpose for the church, noting how it was created to both protect and promote the gospel. The church is God's idea and it's been part of His plan for all of history all along. Let's begin right there, shall we?

God's Plan: God's glory through a people

From the beginning of time the church has been God's idea to bring Himself glory and praise. He has been about making a people for Himself. He declared in Isaiah they are, 'my chosen people,

---

1   Clowney, Edmund, *The Church,* (Downers Grove, IL: IVP, 1995) p.72

2   Duncan, Ligon, Opening endorsements for Mark Dever, *The Church.*

the people whom I formed for myself that they might declare my praise,' (Isa. 43:21). God's eternal plan has always been to display His glory not just through individual people but through a corporate body. The church is not a man-made concept or social structure. It isn't some kind of therapy group for weak people. It's not a club or cultural norm for society. The church is God displaying His glory through a people. The church is, and always has been, God's plan for the revelation of His glory and name. But how can I say that? Where in Scripture do we actually see this idea of the church being God's plan? Keep reading!

The church is the collection of God's chosen people, called by His grace, through faith in Christ and set apart to glorify Him together in the world.[3] The church is a gathered people, it isn't a thing. Sure, a church usually meets in a building, but the building is not what God means when He refers to His body. His body is His chosen people, a people for Himself (1 Pet. 2:9-10). When we talk about the church we aren't fundamentally referencing where they meet, rather, we are referring to the gathering of God's people. It's helpful to think about the church not primarily as a *what*, but a *who*. It's a living organism. So when we ask the question, 'What is the church?' what we should really be asking is, 'Who is the church?'

To help us better understand where we see this in Scripture, let's briefly walk through what the theologians call the *redemptive storyline of the Bible*. This is the story of God's plan for history as displayed to the world. The story of how He has saved a people for Himself through the blood of His own Son. Here we can see firsthand how the church has been His idea since the beginning and continues even today.

OLD TESTAMENT PEOPLE OF GOD

The story starts in the Old Testament and continues to unfold beautifully as we walk through the entirety of the Old Testament

---

3   Ephesians 2:8-9, 19-22, 3:10, 21

and into the New Testament where Jesus visibly comes onto the scene. It began in the garden in Genesis 1 when God created humanity in His image. In Genesis 2:19 God gave Adam the charge of naming every living creature and in 2:23 he even named 'woman,' the complementary image bearer given to him by God. After the fall in the Garden of Eden we read Adam named her more specifically, 'Eve' (Gen. 3:20). Adam and Eve weren't created solely for one another. They were created by God and for God, but the wicked deceiver slithered his way onto the scene and sin entered the world, causing that fellowship to be broken. This problem of separation from God because of sin would plague humanity for thousands of years. And the question looms, 'How will fellowship ever be restored?'

Because of their sin, Adam and Eve were expelled from paradise and learned to live in a fallen world outside the garden. God gave them children, establishing them as a family unit. And as we continue to move through redemptive history in the Old Testament, we see God putting people and families into a larger 'family.' Noah and his wife, his sons and their wives were placed by God in the ark and saved from the flood (Gen. 8:13-19). God then established a covenant to protect them as His people (Gen. 9:1-16). Abraham was also brought into a covenant with God, and God promised to make him a father of a great nation (Gen. 17:5-6). God 'chose' him to lead this group of people (Gen. 18:19). We know this great nation as the people of Israel (Gen. 32:28). Throughout the rest of the Old Testament we come across the phrase, 'my people'[4] repeatedly.

God demonstrated His authority through the naming of His people. Whether or not you have had to name a pet or maybe a child, we can all understand the importance of a name. Naming our first child felt like a rite of passage into parenthood. But why is a name so important? It shows the authority of the one doing

---

4   Exodus 5:1, 6:7, 2 Chronicles 7:14, Jeremiah 30:22, Amos 9:14

the naming, but it also does something else. Naming gives identity. A 'what' becomes a 'who.' No longer 'baby,' but 'Amy.' No longer 'doggie,' but 'Wallace.' So too when God set His love on His people, He designated them 'my people,' thus declaring they are not just any people, but *His* people. It's the repeated phrase Moses says to Pharaoh, 'Let **my** people go, so they may worship me.'[5] His people were set apart to worship Him, but they could not because they were enslaved. They needed a redeemer. God used Moses to be that redeemer for His people in Egypt, leading them out into the wilderness towards the promised land.

The people of God were a nation among the nations, but they were not to live like the nations. They were set apart and expected to keep God's laws, living together in such a way that the character of God was on display through their life together. The laws they kept separated them and marked them out as God's possession. They were to be distinct. That was their job. God had chosen them and set them apart to represent Himself to the world. On Mt. Sinai in Exodus 24, God established a covenant with His people simply because they were *His* people. The covenant was a promise from God to them, sealed by blood, declaring them as His own, and His people vowed they too would keep the covenant and be His people.

> Then he took the Book of the Covenant and read it in the hearing of the people. And they said, 'All that the LORD has spoken we will do, and we will be obedient.' And Moses took the blood and threw it on the people, and said, 'Behold, the blood of the covenant that the Lord has made with you in accordance with all these words.' (Exod. 24:7-8)

But herein lies the problem. They couldn't do it. Just as Adam and Eve sinned in the garden, so the people of God sinned and rebelled against their Creator, breaking their promise to obey all that the Lord had spoken for them to do. The sin that so easily entangled

---

5   Exodus 7:16, 8:1, 8:20, 9:1, 9:13, 10:3, emphasis mine

them could never be fully paid for by their puny sacrifices. They couldn't keep all the words of the Lord as they promised they would. Their sins would require a sacrifice. And yet the bloody sacrifices of bulls and lambs were only temporary fixes. The outlook was bleak for the nation of Israel. But God. He had a plan for His people. He promised them that a Messiah, a Savior, a Redeemer,[6] would come to rescue them fully and finally, forever sealing them to Himself as His special people.

NEW TESTAMENT PEOPLE OF GOD

I find some of the greatest books are the ones with a plot twist so tight it leaves you scratching your head and saying, 'What a minute. How could I have missed all that? I need to read it all over again!' We think we have all the information until our view is expanded and a fuller picture is painted for us to see the whole landscape. Our initial vantage point seems pretty straight forward, until the lens is widened on the horizon of the storyline. Ian McEwan's novel, *Atonement* made me gasp at the end. Learning about Mr. Rochester's past in Charlotte Brontë's *Jane Eyre* brought so many pieces of the plot together. The classic movie plot twist of *Sixth Sense* is still one of the best of all time. It's not that I didn't understand what was happening all along in these stories. I just didn't have the *whole* story. Like trying to interpret a puzzle only half assembled, it's not until every piece is put into place that the entire picture can be seen. When we read the New Testament and the Old Testament together, we widen our theological lenses and better understand God's plan for history and who are His chosen people.

After 400 very silent years of history, the New Testament opens up with a boom, declaring that Jesus is the long-awaited Messiah, the Christ that had been prophesied to come to 'save his people from their sins' (Matt. 1:1,16, 21-23). In a time when Jewish lineages only contained the names of men, Matthew has

---

6   Isaiah 9, 53

the audacity to proclaim the names of women in Jesus' genealogy.[7] Not only are women included, but these were Gentile women who were seen as sexually scandalous. Jesus, the Son of David, the Son of Abraham, the long-awaited King was being connected to sinfulness and scandal. What was happening here? Was Matthew going for a shock effect?

Matthew is simply widening the camera lens for us to see more of the whole redemptive plan set in place at the very beginning, a plan that included a broader swath of people than just the Israelites. There had been whispers in the Old Testament stories that 'not all who descended from Israel belong to Israel' (Rom. 9:6). We read about Gentiles who were brought in among them (Josh. 6:25, Ruth 4:13-21). Women like Rahab and Ruth had become part of God's people. But right here in Matthew chapter 1, the genealogy loudly declares His people are no longer distinguished as ethnically uniform, but now as ethnically diverse,[8] all according to God's original plan to draw people from every tongue, tribe, and nation (Gen. 12:1-3, Rev. 7:9, 14:6).

The New Testament unpacks God's plan for the nations and His church. We watch Jesus upend the understood norm of Jewish centrality among God's elect. Jesus regularly heals, spiritually and physically, those 'outside the camp,' the Gentiles. Mark 7:24-30 where Jesus exorcises a demon from the daughter of a persistent Syrophoenician woman and then commends her for her faith highlights this very thing. Paul understood this and states it clearly in Romans 1:16 saying, 'For I am not ashamed of the gospel, for it is the power of God for salvation to everyone who believes, to the Jew first and also to the Greek.'

Under the old covenant the people of God gathered as an assembly of ethnically Jewish people to worship Him together. But God established a new covenant. Through the life and sacrificial

---

7   Matthew 1:3, 5-6

8   See also Galatians 3:28; 2:11-21; Colossians 3:11; Revelation 5:9

death of His Son, Jesus, He fulfilled the covenantal promises made with His people in the Old Testament and ushered in the new covenant that would include all peoples. Jesus lived the perfect life we could not live and died the death we deserve as sinners. This marked a unique shift in history for all time.

Hebrews 9:15 reads, 'Therefore, he is the mediator of a new covenant, so that those who are called may receive the promised eternal inheritance, since a death has occurred that redeems them from the transgressions committed under the first covenant.' The people of God are no longer set apart ethnically, but spiritually, as those in-dwelt by the Holy Spirit. The new covenant isn't entered into biologically, but supernaturally, through the regenerating work of the Spirit. So where the old covenant was ethnically pure but more spiritually mixed, the new covenant is ethnically mixed and yet spiritually pure.

When John the Baptist prophesied about Jesus, the coming Messiah, he described His power, but also His purpose – that the Holy Spirit would one day indwell His people. 'I baptize you with water for repentance, but he who is coming after me is mightier than I, whose sandals I am not worthy to carry. He will baptize you with the Holy Spirit and fire' (Matt. 3:11). John prophesied the indwelling that would come on the day of Pentecost, when the Holy Spirit was poured out on His people, the church. Like the birth of Jesus, it was a one-time event with eternal ramifications.

It's this ushering in of the Holy Spirit into the hearts of these believers that marks the 'birthday' of the church. G. E. Ladd helpfully unpacks this idea stating, 'The Church properly speaking had its birthday on the day of Pentecost, for the church is composed of all of those who, by one Spirit, have been baptized into one body (1 Cor. 12:13), and this baptizing work of the Spirit began on the day of Pentecost.'[9]

---

9   G. E. Ladd, *The Gospel of the Kingdom,* (Grand Rapids, MI: Eerdmans, 1959) p.117

As we read through the whole of the New Testament we learn how deeply Jesus cares for His church. In fact, He is the one who founded it. In Matthew 16:18 Jesus says, 'And I tell you, you are Peter, and on this rock I will build **my** [emphasis mine] church, and the gates of hell shall not prevail against it.' In fact, Acts 20:28 says that the church of God was, 'obtained with his own blood.' And Ephesians 5:25-6 (NIV) says that 'Christ loved the church and gave himself up for her to make her holy.'

Jesus intimately identifies with the church. So much so that when He confronted Saul during Saul's rampage of persecution against the Christians in Acts 9 He used a personal pronoun when referring to the church saying, 'Saul, Saul, why are you persecuting **me** [emphasis mine]?....I am Jesus, whom you are persecuting.' Jesus considers the church His own body. He founded it, bought it with His blood, and identifies with the church as His very own self. This love is the foundational truth behind the gospel.

RECONCILED TO GOD AND ONE ANOTHER

What is astonishing to see is that God not only reconciled individual people to Himself, but also to one another. He creates a people for Himself. 1 Peter 2:10 says, 'Once you were not a people, but now you are God's people; once you had not received mercy, but now you have received mercy.' And He unifies those people. Ephesians 2:22, 'In him you are also being built **together** [emphasis mine] for God's dwelling in the Spirit.' This new community of people is what God calls the church (Eph. 3:10, CSB).

No longer connected to each other ethnically, the people of God are now connected to one another spiritually and covenantally. The beautiful manifestation of that truth is that our spiritual unity in our ethnic diversity highlights God's beautiful design for His body.[10] It is God's idea for the church to be a people who gather,[11] to be those

10   1 Corinthians 12:12-14

11   Hebrews 10:24-25

brought into fellowship with one another to love and serve God together. God has loved His people from eternity and the pattern He set forth with Israel is the pattern for us today.

Universal versus Local

To understand more about who the church is, there are a couple of distinctions that would be worth our time to consider. The church is often referred to as being 'universal' and 'local.' One of these words refers to time and the other refers to location. But what really is the difference between the church universal and the local church? Are they just two different words to describe the same thing? If not, how are the two related?

Let's break this down just a bit.

Immediately before Jesus' ascension into heaven we read His great commission to go and make disciples of 'all nations,' (Matt. 28:18). The early church, in their ministry of preaching the Word, did indeed obey this command by taking the message of salvation to the ends of the earth. Think about the Ethiopian eunuch in Acts 8 or the Holy Spirit being poured out upon the Gentiles in Acts 10 or Paul's description of the Gentile inclusion in Ephesians 2. In the concluding book of the Bible, Revelation 7:9 we read:

> After this I looked, and behold, a great multitude that no one could number, from every nation, from all tribes and peoples and languages standing before the throne and before the Lamb, clothed in white robes with palm branches in their hands, and crying out with a loud voice, 'Salvation belongs to our God who sits on the throne, and to the Lamb!'

This is the universal church! These are the chosen people of God, from all time, gathered together before the throne singing praises to the King of Kings. *The **universal church** is all true believers from all time until the end of time.* That includes both Old Testament and New Testament believers as planned from before time. A special people, chosen by God, to be with Him forever. The universal church has never been assembled, but one day it will assemble in glory! This universal church is the church comprised of those elect from every nation, from all time, who will gather together before the throne praising the Lord and casting our crowns at His feet (Rev. 4:10). What a glorious thought!

And here's the ringer of it all: God not only created a people for Himself that spans the whole of time, but He placed His chosen people into distinct periods of time. Why? In order to represent Him as a particular people in that time. *These particular people gathering together in a particular time and particular place are what makes up the **local church**.* The universal church is comprised of all these particular people throughout all time. The local church is where our life in the new covenant community gets lived out. Every local church is an expression or manifestation of the universal church.

A DISPLAY OF THE GOSPEL

In today's commitment-phobic world we find many Christians who claim to be a part of the universal church without formally committing themselves to the local church. They may hop around to different churches depending on who happens to be preaching, how much their kids like the youth group, who's leading music, what place offers the best children's ministry. For others their busy schedule with life may have them at home any given Sunday, listening to a podcast of a sermon or inspirational talk and singing a hymn or praise tune before moving along with their day. We have well-intentioned family members who shirk any kind of institutionalized structures and choose to simply 'do church' at home. But is this what God had in mind for His church?

The local church is God's idea for displaying the gospel to the world today. When we commit ourselves to a local congregation of believers and gather Sunday after Sunday we proclaim our Lord's death and resurrection together to the watching world in our time.

Our weekly gatherings are meant to picture that future Revelation gathering of the church universal. You can't belong to the universal if you're not joined to a local, because it's in the local church where we 'put on' our membership in the universal. Without the local church we are in effect without the gospel witness. God has always been about His glory and His reputation as tied to a ***particular*** people. This gospel witness of the church is God's idea.

Just as God marked off Old Testament Israel as a distinct people, a special nation for Himself, the story continues. God intends that distinction of being marked off from the world to characterize the local church. Being a part of the universal church simply isn't enough. The entire New Testament is filled with letters to local churches.[12] These churches knew their sheep, and those sheep carried out their duties and responsibilities to one another because they were a part of the same family of believers.

The church is not an accidental by-product of the gospel, it is essential to the gospel. It is the corporate witness of all God has done for His people in Christ. If it *is* God's idea, we Christians better get it right. Why? Because *the church lies at the very center of the eternal purposes of God*. God doesn't save men and women into the world. God saves men and women into churches. Gospel work in the hearts of God's people creates a real, tangible community, a family, a body. The gospel is church-shaped.[13]

The local church is the authority on earth Jesus has instituted to make known this gospel mystery to the world. How can I make this kind of statement? It's because of what God says to us in His Word about His church. We touched on Ephesians 2 and 3 earlier. Paul,

---

12 Romans, 1&2 Corinthians, Galatians, Philippians, Colossians, 1&2 Thessalonians, 1&2 Timothy, Titus, Philemon, James, 1&2 Peter, 1, 2&3 John, Jude are all letters written to encourage and warn the people of God gathered together in churches.

13 Leeman, Jonathan, *Doctrine of the Church,* lecture

in writing to the Church at Ephesus, is explaining this great gospel **mystery** that has been hidden for ages. What is that mystery?

> In him (Jesus) we have redemption through his blood, the forgiveness of our trespasses, according to the riches of his grace, which he lavished upon us, in all wisdom and insight making known to us the *mystery* of his will, according to his purpose, which he set forth *in Christ* as a plan for the fullness of time, to unite all things in him, things in heaven and things on earth. (Eph. 1:7-10, emphasis mine)

The mystery that has been revealed is God's purposeful plan in Christ to unite all things in Him. And Paul continues in chapter 3:6-12:

> This mystery is that the Gentiles are fellow heirs, members of the same body, and partakers of the promise in Christ Jesus through the gospel... To me, though I am the very least of all the saints, this grace was given, to preach to the Gentiles the unsearchable riches of Christ, and to bring to light for everyone what is the plan of the *mystery hidden for ages* in God, who created all things, so that *through the church* the manifold wisdom of God might now be made known to the rulers and authorities in the heavenly places. This was according to the *eternal purpose* that he has realized in Christ Jesus our Lord, in whom we have boldness and access with confidence through our faith in him. (emphasis mine)

He is telling us that the Gentiles are fellow heirs and this gospel message that has been hidden for ages is made known to the Gentiles and to the rulers and authorities in the heavenly places *through the church*! The church reveals the mystery. It is the church that gives all of history meaning because the gospel can be seen lived out, walking around in the lives of her people – people from all kinds of socioeconomic backgrounds, ethnicities, ages, and stages of life. The local church is God's plan to display the gospel to the world.

This is why calling yourself a Christian and not committing to a local church is somewhat like claiming to be married; and, yet, there's no wedding ring, all your pictures are selfies, you're never seen together with anyone and you are regularly found eating dinner out, alone. It would be hard for us to believe you truly loved and prized your husband if that were your life. Our commitment to the local church is evidence of our love and commitment to the Lord Jesus and His glory. As believers we should care deeply about God's fame and reputation. We do this by following His instructions, uniting ourselves to a local church!

INVISIBLE MADE VISIBLE

Just as a church has a universal aspect and a local aspect, likewise it has an invisible aspect and a visible one. *The **invisible church** is the church from God's eyes.* Referred to as the 'true church' it is comprised of those who are truly saved. Those whose names are written in the Lamb's book of life, those who are 'enrolled in heaven,' (Heb. 12:23). They are the ones who make up the invisible church. The reality is that only God knows those who are truly His (2 Tim. 2:19). Only He knows the spiritual state of each person's heart. Those who are *truly* His are members of the invisible church.

*The **visible church** is the church from the world's eyes.* The visible church is the church as it exists on earth. The invisible church comprises the visible church, but not all members of the visible church are members of the invisible church. For only God can rightly distinguish His sheep from the wolves.[14] Sadly, there will always be unbelievers in visible churches, those who claim to belong to God, but whose hearts are far from Him.[15] We are reminded of

---

14 2 Timothy 2:19

15 See Matthew 13:24: The parable of the wheat and the weeds. This parable highlights God's plan to allow the weeds to grow alongside the wheat until the harvest, the day of judgment. See also Matthew 25:31-46 where Jesus teaches the parable of the sheep and the goats.

this truth in 2 Timothy 2:17-18 when Paul discusses Hymenaeus & Philetus swerving from the truth and also in 4:10 when he talks about Demas' love of the world overpowering him to the point of deserting Paul. While unbelievers may be a part of the visible church, they are not a part of the invisible, eternal church of God.

The local church is where the invisible church is made visible to the world. It's where hidden realities become seen by the world. If you think about it, the church is one of the few aspects of Christian theology that can be observed. This means we need to guard the visible witness of the gospel so when someone asks, 'What is God like?' we can confidently say, 'Look at the church.'[16]

God created the church as a vehicle to get His gospel out to the world, so the local church is not a casual place to meet with God when we feel like it or to have some kind of spiritual experience. The church wasn't created for us to have our needs met. If you are a believer in the Lord Jesus, you are given a job in the local church! You are meant to be a part of this vehicle to display the gospel message of hope to a lost world.

As we've previously noted, the church is God's idea to set apart a people for Himself. The invisible and visible churches are a 'who' not a what, a people not a thing. So a church may call themselves University Baptist Church or The Church on the Hill, but this isn't referencing a building. It's referencing a gathered people of God. The church may meet in a building with a majestic steeple, or it may meet in a high school gym, or it may meet under a designated tree. It's a collective group of individuals, set apart, acting like a billboard advertisement about God. It is a body of believers covenanted together as a visible witness to the world of the gospel. The local church is where the gospel is made visible. The gospel message is the advertisement on the billboard and the church is the display holding up that message. The gospel is the message and

16   We'll discuss this more in chapter 7, *A Flock with a Job to Do*

the church is where that message is displayed, as God's people are formed by His Word and love one another.

If you care about the gospel, you should care about the church. The visible images God gives us in His Word for His people are corporate in nature: branches on a vine, sheep in a fold, parts of a body, members of a household, fellow citizens.[17] God intends for us to be a part of a church in order for the world to 'see' His love displayed through a people. And if the local church is where God intends to make the gospel visible to the world today and you call yourself a believer in the Lord Jesus, why would you risk undermining that witness by not committing to a church? Like a soldier without an army, you cannot fight a war on your own. 'A Christian without a church is a Christian in trouble.'[18] Will you risk treating so lightly what God treats so seriously? God has not abandoned His church, will you?[19]

God's Purpose for the Church: Proclamation

Rosaria Butterfield, a former lesbian and professor of queer theory at Syracuse University was radically converted through the life and ministry of an ordinary pastor and his wife. She understands firsthand the importance of the corporate Christian life and the power of the church's witness to promote the gospel. She emphatically states, 'We are nonnative speakers in this new world culture. We must build strong Christian infrastructure and launch from these.'[20] We are like tiny little lights scattered all around our cities, doing the work God has given us to do and when we gather

---

17   John 15:1-5, John 10:14-16, 1 Corinthians 12:12-14, 2:19-20

18   Leeman, Jonathan and Hanse, Collin; *Rediscover Church,* (Wheaton, IL: Crossway, 2021)

19   We will discuss church membership more fully in Chapter 3, 'A Roaring Fire'

20   Butterfield, Rosaria, *The Gospel Comes with a House Key,* (Wheaton, IL: Crossway, 2018) p. 42

together as a corporate body on a Sunday morning, we shine the light of Christ with a blaze of glory.

Churches act as little kingdom outposts in the world, or embassies in a foreign land. Want to know what true Christianity is? Look at the local church! This is how missions work happens and continues. Without local churches as these outposts we run the risk of losing the true gospel witness to the next generation. The world needs to see these outposts to understand who the people of God are and what they believe. How is that? you might ask.

In Matthew 16:18, Peter confesses to Jesus that Jesus is indeed the Christ. Jesus responds to this confession saying, 'You are Peter, and on this rock I will build my church and the gates of hell shall not prevail against it. I will give you the keys of the kingdom of heaven...'

There is a lot we could discuss in this small section of Scripture, some of which has caused wars and revolutions in history! But for the purposes of this book I want us simply to see two things: the 'who' and the 'what' of the gospel. Peter is given the authority to declare on behalf of Jesus first *who* are truly His, and second *what* the gospel truly is. Matthew 18 then makes it clear (in a case of sin within the church needing to be confronted) that the authority given to Peter is also extended to the local church. In effect, Jesus gave the keys of the kingdom to the church. He gave them a job. We can see this played out when the apostle Paul exhorts the Corinthian church to 'purge the evil person from among you' (1Cor. 5:13). He understood it was the ***church's*** responsibility to exercise the authority of the 'who' and 'what' of the gospel. The keys of the kingdom are the keys of the gospel:

Who: true gospel professors

What: true gospel profession

The church's job is to tell the world **who** belongs to God and **what** is the gospel. In 1 Tim 3:1-15 we read specific qualifications for overseers and deacons, the two biblical offices of the church.

These offices give structure to the church. Paul writes these instructions to Timothy because the church of the living God is 'a pillar and buttress of truth.' This means that the very structure of the church is for the proclamation and protection of the truth, the gospel. A pillar holds the truth of the gospel up on display and the buttress protects and supports that truth. This leads us to our second purpose for the church: protection.

God's Purpose for the Church: Protection

This authority given to the church is not only for the proclamation of the gospel but also for its protection. If you don't know what you believe to be true, how can you protect the truth? If the church corporately protects the gospel witness then each individual's understanding of the Scriptures matter. As the Word dwells richly among us, we sharpen and encourage one another with the truth, both proclaiming it to one another, but also protecting it. It is imperative for us each to individually arm ourselves with the truth of God's Word so together we recognize when an untruth is in our midst. The better we understand the true gospel, the more we'll recognize a false one.

In the United States, Federal agents are trained to spot counterfeit currency through extensive training in genuine currency. They feel, examine and smell the real thing, becoming familiar with every detail. Some are so well versed in the real thing, they can spot a fake blindfolded. By studying the bills intently, the false ones become obvious. Just as training in counterfeit currency begins with studying true currency, knowing the truth of God's Word helps us spot false teaching when it enters the church.

It's why understanding theology and Christian doctrine matters for all members. It's why this book series by women for women is such an invaluable resource. It's why a statement of faith, a set of beliefs held in agreement by the members, is fundamental to all local churches today. We need to know and understand the truths about God and His Word in order to protect the gospel witness. The keys of the kingdom were given to us by God Himself, so we have a job to do in protecting and promoting the gospel in the church.

If we are governed more by the culture and less by the Word of God, we run the risk of being deceived because we don't recognize counterfeits. This is often how cultural relativism slowly seeps into churches, ruining their witness. This is not to say we should be uninformed about the culture we live in. It is to say we must prioritize our understanding of the truth *over* things like cultural fads or norms. Issues like lighting and sound or whether or not there's a pulpit or overhead projectors become less significant than whether or not the gospel is present in the service. The better we understand the surpassing value of the gospel, the less we'll be prone to wander and drift with every passing fad and fancy. We'll have a mooring, a permanent anchor. We may get pushed by culture, but we won't get taken out to sea. Without firm biblically-grounded convictions, the church runs the risk of looking more like a country club, a self-help group, or a community activist association rather than a saved people bonded together over the gospel of Jesus Christ. As Jonathan Leeman put it:

> The local church is the embassy representing Christ's rule across (all) time. The individual Christian does not possess the keys of the kingdom by him or herself. He or she possesses them jointly with the entire congregation.[21]

The purpose of the church is to picture the gospel by proclaiming it to, and protecting it from, the world around her. An embassy is a helpful picture for us to see, not only the church's role, but even our own personal role within her. We are ambassadors for Christ. We represent Him. As a people of God, we have a purpose as a whole that comes to fruition when we fulfill our purposes as

---

21   J. Leeman, *Baptist Foundations: Church Government for an Anti-Institutional Age,* (Nashville, TN: Broadman & Holman Publishers, 2015) p. 360.

individuals within that whole. It is the job of the whole church, leaders and members, collectively and individually, to protect and proclaim the gospel of Jesus Christ. Local churches act as an outpost for the gospel, little embassies on street corners in every country all around the world declaring, 'Jesus is Lord, come inside and see what He looks like!'

THE COSMIC DRAMA OF REDEMPTION

You've heard it said, 'hindsight is always 20/20.' Looking back things seem so much clearer. My understanding of the church wasn't very clear when I was growing up. I had biblical instincts, but lacked the ability to connect the dots. I knew in my head that church was important and loved the church in my heart, but when my college roommates made their comments about going to church on Sunday, I didn't know how to respond. Today I am able to articulate and understand those convictions more fully in order to share them with others, including our children and other women in my life. I marvel at the gift we've been given by God in the local church, even with her flaws and failings. The church has been given the distinct privilege of preaching the 'unsearchable riches of Christ' to a watching world, 'so that through the church the manifold wisdom of God might now be made known to the rulers and authorities in the heavenly places' (Eph. 3:8,10).

As theologian John Stott said reflecting on this verse:

> It is as if a great drama is being enacted. History is the theatre, the world is the stage, and church members in every land are the actors. God himself has written the play, and he directs and produces it. Act by act, scene by scene the story continues to unfold. But who are the audience? They are the cosmic intelligences, the principalities and powers in the heavenly places. We are to think of them as spectators in the drama of

salvation...Thus the history of the Christian church... becomes a graduate school for angels.[22]

The church is a divine idea. It's God's idea. As God's one and only Son, Jesus loved His church so much that He came into the world to die for her, fully and finally securing her to Himself for all eternity. Now she lives as a witness to the world of what God is like and what He has done. The redemptive storyline of the Bible has Jesus, and His bride, the church, as the pinnacle of all history.

22   John R .W. Stott, *The Message of Ephesians* (Downers Grove, IL: Inter-Varsity Press, 1979), pp. 123-124.

QUESTIONS

'A DIVINE IDEA: GOD'S PLAN & PURPOSE FOR THE CHURCH'

God has a plan and a purpose for the church. The church is and has been God's idea to protect and proclaim His glory to the world through a people, His people. As a display of the gospel, the church is where invisible realities are made visible to the world.

1. How would you define the church? Did it just evolve over time? How did it come to be?

2. How is your definition from question 1 similar and/or different from the idea/description you might have had before you started reading this chapter?

3. Compare and contrast the people of God in the Old Testament and the New Testament.

4. What is the difference between the local and universal church? What is the difference between the visible and invisible church?

5. Can someone choose to be a part of the universal or invisible church without bothering with the local church? Why or why not?

6. Paul talks about this great gospel mystery in Ephesians 1:7-10; 3:6-12. Read those passages. What is the great gospel mystery he refers to?

7. What are the two purposes of God's church?

8. Read Matthew 16:13-20. What are the keys of the kingdom? What authority is Jesus giving to Peter?

9. Why is theology not merely for the leaders of the church? Why should we as women study it?

10. If your friend told you she was a Christian but she was too busy for church, how would you explain the importance of church to her?

Chapter 2

A Gathering that Glorifies God:
The Mission of the Church

O Church, arise, and put your armour on;
Hear the call of Christ our Captain.
For now the weak can say that they are strong
In the strength that God has given.
With shield of faith and belt of truth,
We'll stand against the devil's lies;
An army bold, whose battle-cry is Love,
Reaching out to those in darkness.

'O Church Arise'
Stuart Townend & Keith Getty

I wear a lot of hats. I'm not talking about ball caps and straw-brimmed sun shields. Like many women, I have a wide range of duties and responsibilities. So when someone asks me what 'I do,' my response depends on who they are and why they might be asking. Do I mention the often overlooked but invaluable role of being a wife and mother and running a home? How about the volunteer hours preparing Bible study materials or counseling women? Maybe I should mention my nursing job that actually pays an income? When someone poses the question, 'What do you do?' I'm assuming what they want to know is 'Who are you? What drives and excites you?' They're asking, 'What is your purpose in life?'

Every morning we wake up, toss off the covers and put our feet to the ground for a reason, and I'm not referring just to coffee here, although that is of primary importance to the inhabitants of our home! We get out of bed for a reason, a purpose. Whether or not it's a 4:55am wake up cry from a hungry infant, a 5:00 alarm beckoning you back to the hospital or a 6:30 shaking from a parent to get you to class on time, there is a point to your day. God created humans in His image. Then He commanded those humans to work (Gen. 1:28; 2:15). We were created by Him for worship and for work as a means of being His witness to the world. When we look at Scripture, we watch this thread of 'worship, work, and witness' weave it's way through redemptive history. As we discussed in chapter 1, the church is the people of God, created by Him and for Him.[1] So the question before us now is what are her job responsibilities and does God have anything to say about them in His Word?

This is important for us to consider because within the last two decades much ink has been spilled debating the purpose or 'mission' of the church. For some, that means hip coffee and after-school tutoring programs. For others, it means giving more money to global missions. But underlying it all is the question, 'What is the church supposed to do?' What is it's job description?

'Missional' has become a fashionable buzzword within the evangelical community for the past two decades such that 'missional' has become synonymous with 'Christian.' 'Missionary' is often the job description of some in the church. How can we use the word, 'mission' in a way that is consistent with what God says in His Word should be the mission of the church? When we gather as believers

---

1   Exodus 19:5-6

in the Lord Jesus Christ week after week, what is our 'job'? What is the 'purpose' of our gatherings?

Ultimately, we gather for the glory of God's name. The primary and most fundamental purpose of the church is the glorification of the Lord Jesus Christ. We do that through our corporate worship, our ministry to one another in discipleship, and our evangelism to the world. In other words, we glorify God in our worship, our work, and our witness as a means of making disciples.

Hardwired for Worship

As a labor and delivery nurse I am continually amazed at the way God created a baby's longing for safety and warmth to be met simply by keeping that baby's skin against her mother's skin. At birth, when a baby's temperature drops, their blood sugar can become unstable and their breathing rate increases rapidly. One of the first lines of defense we have is to put that baby right up on her mother's chest, next to her beating heart (kangaroo care, as we call it). It is there, next to her mother that she calms and stabilizes. Warmth, care, safety, and even food. These are all the things that a baby needs to transition to life outside the womb. In God's beautiful design, that longing for the mother is what keeps the infant alive. The newborn is instilled with biological hardwiring that draws her to her mother. Her mother is the center of her life.

Just like a newborn is drawn to her mother, we humans were hardwired to be drawn to God. We were created to live with God at the center of our lives. Like a newborn infant, we long to be satisfied and safe. The gnawing and longing we feel in our souls is a longing for the Creator, the God of the universe. But unlike the baby who is kept safe in her mother's arms, we run to false gods and worship them instead. We were originally created for God, but in our sin we are hardwired to run *from* God. Because of sin's entrance into the world, our hearts are drawn away from God towards that which cannot satisfy. We have forsaken God who, as the prophet

Jeremiah says, is 'the spring of living water' and we have dug our own cisterns, 'broken cisterns that cannot hold water' (Jer. 2:13, NIV). In other words, we have turned away from God and turned toward that which cannot fill us. We run after things which leave us empty and hollow inside. We keep looking for satisfaction in things and people all around us, ignoring the one who can fully and completely satisfy us.

We are all worshippers. Whether or not you've considered that truth, it's worth pondering for a moment. From the moment we come into the world we are driven by intense longings that we give and devote ourselves to. It's worship, whether our longings are focused on success, acceptance, comfort, reputation, family, or even our food! We worship things that make us 'feel' complete or whole. Augustine rightly observed, 'Our souls are restless until they find their rest in you.' Those other things will not satiate our cravings. They leave us agitated. We long to worship, but we look in the wrong direction. We are restless in our worship of all these other things that do not give our souls peace. Only the worship of the one true God can truly satisfy and give us rest. God knows this about us. He created us to worship Him and yet, in our sinfulness we run the other direction and seek shelter under the broken wings of empty promises. But from the very beginning of time He was establishing a way for us to fellowship with Him, to find refuge in the shelter of His wings (Ps. 61:4).

In the beginning, God created Eve to be with Adam because 'it was not good that the man should be alone' (Gen. 3:18). He created the one for the other so they might worship him together. They were different, but the same. They were complements of one another.[2] Just a few verses later God calls to them as He is walking in the garden in the cool of the day. He is calling them to commune with Him.[3] Adam and Eve were to worship the Lord God together.

---

2   Genesis 2:18, 23

3   Genesis 3:8

But most of you are familiar with how that story went. Adam and Eve rebelled against God and chose to worship created things rather than the Creator Himself thus breaking fellowship with God and one another. But God showed mercy. He covered their nakedness with animal skins. This was the very first sacrifice. As we continue to read on in the Old Testament we see God supply His people with an intercessor, a priest, who, through the blood of bulls and goats, made a way to reunite His people with Him. His people gathered together to celebrate and worship the gift of this forgiveness for their sins. But no amount of animal sacrifice could pay for their rebellion. God would one day send His only Son to this world as the ultimate payment for sins, forever securing His people to Himself. He made a way for His people to be restored to fellowship with Him.

Those restored to fellowship leave false gods and worship the one true and living God. It's not just Adam and Eve who were created to worship together. Over and over again in the Bible we read of the people of God gathering together to worship Him in the tent of meeting (Exod. 40:34) and the tabernacle in the wilderness (Num. 9:15); to give praise together in the house of the Lord (Luke 4:16); to worship by listening to God's Word read in synagogues (Luke 4:16); and pray and sing together in newly formed house churches (Acts 8:3). God's people have always *gathered together* for the express purpose of corporate worship through the reading, singing, and praying of the Word. It is no different for us Christians today. When we gather week after week we are declaring with one voice and heart that Jesus is alive and is coming back to bring His people home. We gather together to worship the King of all Kings and the Lord of all Lords, *together*! We are giving Him due praise as our risen and reigning King. It is even commanded in Hebrews 10:25 to not neglect meeting together.

GLORIFY GOD AND ENJOY HIM TOGETHER

God has prescribed how He is to be worshipped when we do gather together. His Word is to be central in it all, whether reading, singing, or praying. We'll delve more into the particulars of these components in chapter 4, but for our purposes here, I want you to understand the primary purpose of the gathering. Ephesians 1:12 tells us we were made for 'the praise of his glory.' The Westminster shorter catechism helpfully begins, 'The chief end of man is to glorify God and enjoy him forever.' And this is what we do corporately, whether it's Adam and Eve, the people of Israel, or the gathering of local churches. We might be helped to amend the catechism ever so slightly to say, 'the chief end of man is to glorify God and enjoy him *together*.' The chief end is a collection of people glorifying God and enjoying Him. The primary purpose of the corporate gathering is the worship of the Lord Jesus Christ *together* for the express purpose of bringing Him glory. We do not gather simply for ourselves or even others. That, as we'll discuss in a moment, is a vitally important part of the gathered worship, but the ultimate and singular purpose of a Sunday morning gathering of believers is to bring praise, glory, and honor to God. We gather as a church body to pursue the glory of God over the glory of self. Ephesians 2:22 tells us we are 'built together into a dwelling place for God by the spirit.'

Colossians 3:16 tells us, 'Let the word of Christ dwell in you richly, teaching and admonishing one another in all wisdom, singing psalms, and hymns and spiritual songs, with thankfulness in your hearts to God.' There's a 'one another' component to our worship. When we stand together on any given Sunday and glance across the faces of our brothers and sisters worshipping and praising God, we behold the beauty of their worship and are reminded that we worship a great God and not ourselves. We are spurred on, and spur others on, to deeper worship, giving all the glory to God. This worship becomes a ministry to one another as well as to the world.

Work: Better Together

I enjoy watching movies like *Saving Private Ryan* or *1917*. It's inspiring
to watch relationships form between complete strangers who
come together to work for a common purpose and goal. They are
defending themselves against a common enemy and protecting one
another's lives with their own. Some of the best stories of history
are the ones that involve individuals who were formerly strangers
and even enemies, coming together for the good of others. Think
of the Underground Railroad, or the Ten Boom family's community
that hid Jewish families during the holocaust. It took groups of
people working together to combat whatever evil or hardship they
were facing. There's power in working together.

We like these stories because we can identify with them.
Community is in our DNA. God created us for it. From Adam
and Eve, to Israel, to the church today, God has infused us with
an internal longing to be a part of a group with a shared identity
and focus. Today, the church is the community God has given us
to work together for the common goal of glorifying Him. In the
beginning Adam was charged with working and watching over the
garden.[4] Israel was to work in, and watch over, the Promised Land.
Today we work and watch over God's church. When we work to
encourage, protect, build up, guard, and invest in one another, we
grow corporately, not just individually. It is through that corporate
witness that we declare the goodness of God to the world.

In the Old Testament, God's people gathered together to display
God's faithfulness and loyalty to His people as well as His lordship
over all. They were set apart as a community that represented
God's holiness to the world through their individual and corporate
holiness. They were a distinctive group with the common goals of
glorifying God and growing in holiness. In a practical sense, we
can see how desperately we need one another. Part of the reason
we enjoy team sports, group exercise classes, knitting or, book

---

4   Genesis 2:15

clubs, and community service groups, is because of this need for community. We were meant to live together and cooperate with others. Those clubs and groups demonstrate the way we were made to come together for a shared purpose.

As Christians, we gather together every week to declare the goodness of God to Him and to one another! We praise Him and give Him glory as individuals and as a collective whole. Our corporate community not only brings glory to God and acts as a witness to the world, but is a tangible encouragement to the individuals within that community. We work to encourage one another to fight the good fight, run the race marked out for us. We work to build one another up to seek the *good portion* of Jesus Himself. We work to remind one another of the hope we have in heaven when the days of struggle seem to have no end. This is what it looks like to truly love one another. We gather as a ministry to one another! The young parent struggling with restless kids in the pew needs the encouragement of the more seasoned parents leading their children in a Sunday morning service. The single can be encouraged and challenged by the widow or widower worshipping God despite what they don't have. The closet binge drinker sees the one who's now been sober for a decade, and beholds a picture of hope and change. We work for one another's good, for the glory of God alone.

We will discuss more specifically the responsibilities and privileges of this corporate life a little in our next chapter and more fully in chapter 8. For our purposes here, I want us to see the 'why' along with the 'what' as the point of church. The bottom line is that we need one another. We need others and others need us. *Church isn't a building we sometimes visit or a service we occasionally observe – it's a family to whom we belong.* And it's our working together as a spiritual family that makes the biggest wave of impact in our communities. Our life together is meant to edify and build each other up in Christ, to shine His love like a brilliant light to the world.

KNOW BEFORE YOU SERVE

It takes work to get to truly know people. In our membership classes at church we encourage new members to delay serving in more practical/visible ways in the church for the first few months after they join. There can be excitement and eagerness to get going with the ministry life happening all around. That is a wonderful instinct! We don't want to discourage anyone in that excitement, but instead we want to channel it towards knowing and loving their new church family more than just serving them practically. We encourage them to use their time and energy in getting to know their brothers and sisters and to sit under the regular preaching and teaching of God's Word, singing and praying that Word together with their new family.

While eagerness to get involved in 'hands on' ministry is commendable, it's imperative to grow in knowledge and love of those with whom you are serving. Doing so allows them to learn more fully what it looks like to be a follower of Jesus with other people. As individual relationships grow, they are able to sharpen one another as 'iron sharpens iron' (Prov. 27:17). They are able to carry out their duties as a church member more fully to one another as they grow to know and understand them. Taking time for fellowship fosters love for one another and God Himself who brought us together, and gives us a fuller understanding of how God might use us in our particular church in our particular season of life. It sets the stage for individual members to do what God has called us to do in the great commission: make disciples!

IRON SHARPENING IRON

One of my favorite types of meme to watch usually involves a small child mimicking a parent. The copycatting of behaviors is not only comedic and entertaining, but the similarities are often remarkable. As a mother I know how profoundly my behavior, speech, mannerisms, and habits are imitated by my own children.

Early on in my parenting adventure, I dropped something really heavy and sharp onto my foot causing the skin to break and start bleeding. Without showing any restraint I cried out, 'Oh, crap!' To my horror, my two-year-old little girl was standing nearby and walked away from the scene of the crime singing, 'oh crab, oh crab, oh crab....' I was mortified. One little verbal hiccup and she caught it! Well, at least sort of caught it. I was grateful to hear her refer to the sea creature in her mishearing and not my crassness. Oh, what little sponges children can be. By default they often absorb these mannerisms. But if we're honest, that's how every single human can be.

Point being – we're all followers. In fact the word 'disciple' simply means follower. Which means we're all disciples, we're all followers of someone or something. What makes a Christian distinct is that they follow Christ. This individual act of following Christ is what we call _discipleship_. It speaks to the vertical relationship between a Christian and her Savior.

Yet Jesus gave His followers a job description. They're not just to be disciples, they're to work to _make disciples_. The gospels of Matthew, Mark, and Luke all close with a variation of the same teaching, what we refer to as the Great Commission. In the Bible, one's last words carry special weight (e.g. Moses, Joshua, David).[5] So it is with Jesus. In that commission He empowers His followers with His authority to 'go, therefore, and make disciples of all nations, baptizing them in the name of the Father and of the Son and of the Holy Spirit, teaching them to observe everything I have commanded you' (Matt. 28:18-20).

The controlling verb is 'make disciples'. Going, baptizing, and teaching describe _how_ the disciples are to be made. So what is the mission of the church? Very simple: make disciples. That shouldn't come as any big surprise for it's exactly what Christ did. It's exactly what He commanded His followers to do. It's what we see Paul

---

5   Deuteronomy 33, Joshua 24:19-28, 1 Kings 2:1-9

do through His own letters and ministry. The church's mission is disciple-making.

This means the work of the church is primarily about people. *People* remain the focus more than structures, organizations or institutions. That's not to say ministries meant to promote justice or relieve physical suffering are unimportant. They can provide a wonderful entree to share the gospel as we let our light shine before others (Matt. 5:16). Yet as much as we want to relieve *temporal* suffering, what the church is uniquely called to do is relieve *eternal* suffering.[6] And we do that in our churches by making disciples. Which means we must *go* to the lost, *baptize* them (which implies the gospel has been preached and they've repented of their sins and been brought into God's family (Acts 2:38, 41), and then *teach* them to obey all Christ has commanded. It's clear Jesus isn't just interested in decisions. He wants mature disciples who are making disciples.

If you've ever had a blunt kitchen knife you know how frustrating it can be. It is unable to do the job for which it was created. But in order to make the knife sharp again it requires friction. That cannot happen alone. The knife must be pressed and rubbed against another hard surface in order to sharpen its 'teeth.' We need the friction and pressure of rubbing up against other Christians to sharpen us for the work God has for His servants (Prov. 27:17). As the late preacher, C.H. Spurgeon once said, 'God's swords must be used.' And if we are meant to be used, we must be sharp for use. We gather as a church to sharpen one another in our own personal holiness and in our evangelism. We need one another in order to be sharpened.

6   Kevin DeYoung and Greg Gilbert's book, *What is the Mission Of the Church?* (Wheaton, IL: Crossway, 2011) is a vital resource on this topic. They helpfully note, '[T]here is something worse than death and something better than human flourishing. If we hope only for renewed cities and restored bodies in this life, we are of all people most to be pitied' (p.23).

This deliberate act of doing spiritual good for others in order to help them follow Christ is what we call *discipling*. In his book *Discipling*, Mark Dever puts it this way, 'discipling really is just a bunch of church members taking responsibility to prepare one another for glory.'[7] It is the intentional means of doing spiritual good in the life of another believer to encourage them along in their journey home to heaven. So if *discipleship* describes my vertical relationship with Jesus, *discipling* describes how I'm horizontally working to help other people follow Jesus.

But this discipling ministry won't happen without work, the collective work of the church laboring together. For it's here in local churches where we make a commitment to one another and gather under the authoritative teaching of God's Word. If God gave the keys of the kingdom to the local church, as we discussed in depth in chapter 1, then the church is where we can affirm what is the true message of the gospel and who truly professes the gospel. The church provides an accountability for us as we seek to grow as disciples of Christ and help others along as they do the same. The weekly gathering of the saints is a delightful opportunity for us to remind one another of the truth of God and His Word, and spur one another along to run the race of perseverance marked out for each one of us. We act like little Dory from the movie, *Finding Nemo*, but instead of singing 'just keep swimming, just keep swimming,...,' we encourage one another to 'just keep running, just keep running.' When we face struggles with sin or difficult circumstances or persecution, we remind one another to run the race of perseverance set out by the Lord Jesus for us (Heb. 12:1-2). When we build into one another like this, we stoke the fire of both our own and one another's holiness.

The writer of Hebrews exhorts us to, 'watch out' and 'encourage' each other daily 'so none of you is harmed by sin's deception' (Heb. 3:12-13, CSB), and further on in chapter 10 to,

---

7   Dever, Mark, *Discipling* (Wheaton, IL: Crossway, 2016), p.43

'consider one another in order to provoke love and good works, not neglecting to gather together, as some are in the habit of doing, but encouraging each other, and all the more as you see the day approaching' (Heb. 10:24-25, CSB). Right here we see the urgency to be together, gathering, warning, encouraging, and stirring one another up towards the work we have as Christians – corporate edification. This is the kind of work we are to be doing in the church. We are called to encourage one another in the worship of the one true God and display our unity to the world, to warn one another when sin begins to harden and sear our consciences towards God's truths. We are agents to foster and fuel holy growth in the lives of our brothers and sisters. This kind of mutual accountability helps us to watch over one another with brother and sisterly love. Paul tells us in Ephesians 4:15-16, 'we are to grow up in every way into him who is the head, into Christ, from whom the whole body, joined and held together by every joint with which it is equipped, when each part is working properly, makes the body grow so that it builds itself up in love.' We work together, spurring one another on towards love and good deeds, growing in our love and worship of our Lord and Savior. It's been said, 'It takes a village to raise a child, but it takes a church to raise a saint.'

As we grow individually in our love for Jesus, we are better able to grow as a whole in our love for Him. Our love for Jesus overflows into the love for our brother and sister in Christ. Our holiness as a community of believers is affected by each individual of our community. When one suffers, we all suffer. When one grows, we all grow. So in effect, we have an obligation to see to each individual's holiness because of this collective impact. Therefore as we grow in holiness and mature individually, we do so corporately, and that has the greatest impact on our witness to the world.

If the local church is the vehicle God uses to display His glory, then our churches should direct resources, time, and energy to the things most directly connected to Word-ministry and world mission. Our collective efforts as a local body of believers should be focused on planting healthy churches that prioritize this biblical model of discipling. Our mission dollars should be spent investing in people whose purpose is to bring the gospel message to the lost and to establish a faithful gospel witness in a local church.

Witness: A window into our world

One of the strangest things that has come from the social media age is the ability to 'stalk' other people. Just the other day I heard a coworker talking about a guy she was interested in. She nonchalantly said, 'Yeah, I got online and Facebook stalked him. He seems pretty decent.' Facebook, Instagram, Pinterest, Tik-Tok, Linkedin, a myriad of other social media applications: these platforms offer the world a means of discovering information about people. What is displayed online is rarely the whole truth, but it does give us a window into the values, interests, and priorities of the account holder. Whether for dating, employment, or other interests, the online information is a witness to the world of what that person wants you to think they're all about.

As Christians, our lives act like a social media account, broadcasting our beliefs. If we claim the name of Christ, what we post reflects on Him. How we conduct ourselves, what we say, how we say it, and especially how we handle our sin and the sin of those around us, tells a story about Christ. As we walk around this world declaring the truth of the gospel and sharing the hope of Jesus, our lives will either back up or deny our claims. God tells us repeatedly in the New Testament to 'bear fruit in keeping with repentance' (Matt. 3:8). Paul states this very truth in the middle of his testimony to King Agrippa when he says that all men, 'should repent and turn to God, performing deeds in keeping with their repentance' (Acts 26:20). Our repentance is the key initial marker of how we are to be distinct. We are not to be conformed to the things of this world but transformed by the renewing of our minds (Rom. 12:2). We don't live this way in order to be saved, but as a demonstration that we have been saved. The way we live our lives matters. If we're not careful, we may not have truth in our advertising.

But it's not just our individual witness that matters. Our corporate lives magnify and multiply the message of our individual lives. They're like a sponsored social media post, they boost, amplifying our message. It's one thing for us to share our testimony with a coworker, but when they see Christian brothers and sisters in a local church do life together as a people of God they are given a fuller picture of our truth claims. Much like when we meet the family or friends of someone we're dating, we gain a more comprehensive knowledge of who they are and what they really believe about relationships. We weigh in our minds their truth claim to care about us by the way they actually care about the others in their life whom they also say they love. Our claim to love God is backed up when we love our brothers and sisters in Christ. And when they see our brothers and sisters loving us, they want what we have.

So when we gather week after week, we act as a collective witness of God's love for His people in how we worship together. It is a corporate and not just an individual witness. God intended the church to be the manifold witness of God to this world and the heavenly realms![8] Our collective lives are small social media posts gathered together to make one giant post displaying the hope of the gospel message to the world. It's why Jesus says in the book of John, 'By this all people will know that you are my disciples, if you have love for one another' (John 13:35). When one life that has been transformed by the gospel is connected to many other transformed lives, the color is enhanced on our posts. That color enhances the message of each individual who speaks.

Our weekly gathering of worship to God and ministry to one another acts as a witness to the outside observer. The church is

---

8   Ephesians 3:10

where invisible realities are made visible for others to see.[9] When our unbelieving neighbors, friends, or family join us for a church service, they are, in effect, joining us for family dinner. They watch how we interact with one another. They see a college student helping an older widow to her seat. They see a special needs person hugging the people around him and those people look him in the eye, hug him back, and ask how he is doing.

It's worth noting that while our church gatherings are a display of God's love for His people, church isn't primarily an evangelistic rally. We want non-Christians to attend our services and join our meetings so they can see and experience the gospel truths, but the primary purpose of our gatherings is for the believer to fill up with God's truth for the week ahead. Our gathering should be attractional *so far as* we make the gospel attractive by living beautiful, holy lives together. The gospel is the focus of these weekly meetings and should always be taught and never assumed. It's a means to prepare the members to be evangelists to go out of the doors and share the good news of Jesus. As forgetful believers, we need these weekly, repetitive gospel reminders like a water station break along a marathon route. This rhythm of refueling for the weary saint is where we welcome the unbeliever to see, hear, and experience the gospel truths.

EVANGELISM IS A TEAM EFFORT

Not only do unbelievers get a show-and-tell of the gospel story by joining us for our weekly gatherings, but our evangelism out in the world is strengthened when we experience and rehearse the gospel truths together. This love we have for God and one another should naturally overflow into love for the lost. The more we grow in our understanding of God's merciful love for us in Christ Jesus, the more we should want to share that love with others. Part of our discipling of one another should include the encouragement to

---

9   Jonathan Leeman, *Baptist Foundations,* p. 364

share the good news with others. When we encourage one another to grow in personal holiness, we are encouraging each other's growth in personal evangelism. Jesus' last words to His disciples were, 'Go, therefore, and make disciples...'[10] As we work together as a family to encourage one another's spiritual health and growth, we spur one another on to 'Go.'

I have one friend in my church who I'm regularly encouraged and convicted by as I listen to and watch her evangelism and love for the lost. As a busy mother, Hayley prays and strategically considers how to better position herself to share the gospel with her lost friends. But what is so spectacular, is how she includes others from our church in her efforts! Hayley leads by example. She strategically hosts events at her home mixing people from our church with a number of unbelievers. She participates in women's sporting events and trains with believers and unbelievers hoping to spark different conversations. Knowing the burden she carries for these friends, we are able to pray for her and check in to see how things are going. We talk often about things we do or talk about with these people, striving to find more efficient ways to not just live lives of holiness, but open up our mouths to declare the truth of the gospel of Jesus Christ. We have the unique privilege to enhance the message we each individually proclaim as we partner together.

Another way we partner together is in our corporate prayer meetings. We regularly pray for evangelistic opportunities and for the gospel message to bear fruit. For example, we have two members, Jennifer and Rob, who have worked together to coordinate a ministry to children in our city's low-income housing area. Rob has helped in a variety of ways, including bussing kids onto our campus in order to participate in some of our children's ministry and more recently to lead a Bible study for some of the young men. Jennifer has also led a study of God's Word for the young girls and some of the women. As a forty-something single

---

10   Matthew 28:18a

woman, she selflessly gives of her time for these pre-teens and teens with the hope that the gospel seed may land on fertile soil in their hearts. As they partner together, the whole church partners with them in prayer and practical support.

These examples from our own church show the benefit of us working together for the common goal of glorifying and praising God with our mouths and our lives in our evangelistic efforts. When we do, we are better equipped to fight the battles we will undoubtedly face. For our struggle is against the enemy of this dark world and we need the help of our brothers and sisters to fight against the rulers, authorities, and powers of darkness in this world. God built us to wrestle together against the spiritual forces of evil in the heavenly places. We can be picked off if we battle alone. We must work together, encourage one another, defend and pray for one another against the schemes of the devil.[11]

When our churches are filled with people who declare with their mouth Jesus is Lord and believe in their hearts God raised Him from the dead and then work together to proclaim that message in their lives both individually and corporately, a powerful impact is made. Louis Berkof says it well stating, 'Only a Church that is really strong, that has a firm grasp of the truth, can in turn become a powerful missionary agency and win mighty conquests for the Lord. Thus the task of the Church is a comprehensive task. She must point out the way of salvation, must warn the wicked of their coming doom, must cheer the saints with the promises of salvation, must strengthen the weak, encourage the faint-hearted and comfort the sorrowing.'[12] The local church is the vehicle to promote our evangelism. When we do this in our local churches, we strengthen our witness to those who gather among us on any given Sunday and

---

11 Ephesians 6:12

12 Louis Berkof, *Systematic Theology,* (Edinburgh: Banner of Truth.2002), p. 596

we also grow in our encouragement to one another to go and tell the good news of Jesus.

Sabbaths without end

With all the hats I have, the most important one I ever wear is as a disciple of Christ. That is the most important job I hold, and I link arms with others wearing the same hat to do that job. God has clearly spelled out the church's job description. We gather together to declare the goodness of what God has done for us in Christ. Our church services each week prepare us not only for the coming week, but for eternity! The lyrics from the classic old hymn, 'Jerusalem my happy home,' rightly verbalize that longing we have for our heavenly home of worship, 'Oh, when, thou city of my God, shall I, thy courts ascend? Where congregations ne'er break up and sabbaths have no end.' It will be the best of unending worship for the people of God, that Sabbath rest.[13] No coronavirus or government mandate will keep us from that family gathering.

As we wait and anticipate the glorious inheritance before us, we gather together as His people to worship Him, reminding one another of all He has done for us, spurring one another on toward love and good deeds, while declaring and sharing the hope we have to this lost and dying world. We gather to worship the one true God, work to build one another up in holiness, all as a witness to the world. Unbelievers are watching. What is it they will see as they watch us walk these roads to heaven *together* as the people of God?

---

13   Hebrews 4:9

Questions

'A Gathering That Glorifies God: The Mission of the Church'

The church was created to be a gathering of God's people, worshipping Him together and encouraging one another along the road to heaven. When we gather, we build one another up in the Lord, but also in our evangelism as we declare the good news of the gospel together.

1. If the primary purpose of the gathered people of God, the church, is the glorification and praise of the Lord Jesus, how do we go about executing that goal? What must our gathering be based on?

2. Every one of us is a worshipper. What kinds of things do you find yourself worshiping?

3. What can you do to reorder who or what you worship this next week?

4. What does it look like for you to 'work' in your local church?

5. If discipleship is our vertical, personal relationship with Christ, what is discipling?

6. If you have benefitted from, or are investing in, a discipling relationship, share what things you've done to encourage one another and spur one another on to love and good deeds.

7. Pray and consider who you might be able to pour your life into as a discipling relationship.

8. How might your brothers and sisters assist you in your own personal evangelism? If you are sharing the gospel regularly,

how might you help another sister grow in her evangelistic efforts? What are some things you could do to partner with one another to reach the lost?

9. How does your prayer life reflect a desire to see members of your church go out with the gospel? What would it look like for you to increase your partnership with others in prayer?

Chapter 3

A Roaring Fire:
The Importance and Privilege of Church Membership

O Church of Christ invincible,
The people of the Lord;
Empowered by the Spirit's breath,
And nourished by His word.
His covenant of grace will be Our portion evermore;
For he who called us will not change,
Our help and our reward

'O Church of Christ Invincible'
Matt Boswell

Growing up as a Christian camp junkie, I knew all of the best camp songs. I even had a song book for my piano-practicing days that included the best and most beloved Christian camp tunes of the 1980s and 90s (Really classic stuff!). One of those songs was titled, 'Pass it On'. It begins with the words, 'It only takes a spark to get a fire going.' (I'm really hoping some of you are humming along as you read.) Filled with evocative and individualistic notions of

God's love, the theme is about evangelism. Once we know and experience the love of God, a spark is ignited that fuels a fire of God's love for others to experience . The problem with this image is that a spark fades *unless* it's combined with other sparks to make a fire. Individual sparks may give off a momentary burst of heat, but nothing lasting and nothing in comparison to a roaring fire of collective sparks. As Christians, we need one another to fan the flame of God's love in our hearts so the watching world can feel the collective heat of our sparks together.

The Importance of Church Membership

PICTURES WITH A PURPOSE

God's Word contains numerous images and metaphors for the church. No doubt you've heard the phrase, 'a picture is worth a thousand words.' Well God has done that for us through His own Word when describing His church. These portraits contribute important information that assists our understanding of the church and how we are to relate to her. They are pictures with a purpose. A family, a body, living stones, a sheep, a bride, vine and branches, a field of crops, and a harvest are just a few examples.

It's important for us to allow each of these images to help us interpret the other. Every illustration, even great ones, breaks down in some way if pushed too far and too literally. But looking at them collectively can help us see shared commonalities and repeating themes. Notice, for example, that all of these images I just listed have something in common: plurality! They involve more than one. That's because as Christians we are the people of God, not just a person of God. The Bible teaches church membership through these metaphors for the church because the *gospel creates a community of believers.* Let's take a deeper look at a few of these images and how God's idea for the church, and specifically membership in the local church, is pictured through these illustrations.

THE FAMILY OF GOD

When God's mercy is extended to us we become one of His people. We become a part of His family and He becomes our Father (Rom. 8:15). We are graciously adopted by God (Eph. 1:5) and become members of His household, His covenant community (Gal. 3:27–4:7). But don't forget this crucial bit of information: *our reconciliation with God means reconciliation with His people.* Paul discusses this very thing in Ephesians 2:19-20 when he writes,

> So then you are no longer strangers and aliens, but you are fellow citizens with the saints and members of the household of God, built on the foundation of the apostles and prophets, Christ Jesus himself being the cornerstone.

Sure we are individually reconciled to God, but we are also brought into relationship with a host of other professing believers. So when individuals become believers they don't just exist as individual Christians. They become a part of a new community.[1] We become 'fellow citizens,' 'members of his household' and community, as we just read in Ephesians 2:20.

The Christian life is a family affair. It's not just you and Jesus. It isn't just a random group of people either. We become the body of Christ together, a true family. In 1 Timothy, Paul calls Timothy, 'my true child in the faith,' (1:1) and instructs him to care for other members of the church like family members: fathers, brothers, mothers, sisters (5:1-2). At the end of Romans, Paul sends greetings to individual, local churches in Rome, actually calling them families (16:10, 11). God designed local churches to be families. The depth of relationship shared in a biological family is to signify the depth of relationship we have within our spiritual church families.

Let's rotate this familial image just a little and consider what it means to be adopted into a family. When an orphan is adopted, she

1   Bray, Gerald, *God is Love: A Biblical & Systematic Theology,* (Wheaton, IL: Crossway, 2012) p. 667

is brought into an immediate family, a father and mother, possibly brothers and sisters. These people will care for her, know her, watch out for her and provide for her. She also may gain grandparents, aunts and uncles, and cousins. When conversion happens, God's Word tells us that we are likewise brought into God's family, a family who will care for us, know us, watch out for us, and provide for us. This is exactly how the *local church* should work.[2] When we commit ourselves to a local body we are identifying ourselves with a particular family of believers. These immediate, local church 'families' make up the extended, universal family of believers. In the adoption process, a child isn't brought into an extended family without being a part of the immediate family first. And just like family, we have both immediate relatives and extended relatives. Local churches are somewhat like an immediate family and the universal church is something like our extended family. We know the whereabouts and happenings of our immediate family in greater

---

2   I recognize some of you have been hurt by a local church, disillusioned or confused by things done to you or to those you love. Might I encourage you not to throw the baby out with the bath water and assume all churches are corrupt, separating yourself from the means of grace God has for you through His church? Good authority is loving and patient. It gives to others and doesn't take. Bad authority distorts the good gift from God, using it for evil, often selfish purposes. If that has been your experience, I'm deeply and genuinely sorry. It grieves me to hear stories of betrayal, abandonment, and abuse. Yet God's authority is perfect, and He uses all things to accomplish His purposes, even the hard stuff. We have a very real enemy who seeks to kill, steal, and destroy, especially something as precious as the church, Christ's own body. What Satan would love is for you to allow an evil experience like yours to keep you from the good that God can and promises to do through His church. He would love for you to believe the satanic lie, traced all the way back to the garden, that authority can't be trusted. Our Redeemer isn't finished. He is just and will correct every wrong some day. In the meantime, He is working in and around us through the church, His bride. Don't abandon her, for Christ surely hasn't.

detail than we tend to about our extended family, and our immediate family are the priority in our lives. When they have needs, we try to meet them and vice versa. They're our line of first defense. The local church cares for her members on that immediate family level.

The Old Testament people of God looked more like a biological, monochromatic family, whereas the New Testament people of God are from every tribe, tongue, and nation,[3] looking more like a true blended family. Ryan Lister illustrates this well in his book, *Emblems of the Infinite King: Enter the Knowledge of the Living God,* saying, 'This is a ragtag family made up of all kinds of people with all kinds of pasts and all kinds of circumstances. When we see the church as a whole, it looks like a patchwork quilt, with different shapes, patterns, colors, and designs all sewn together by the thread of faith and the King's steady hand.'[4] This privilege of adoption into God's chosen family allows us to work together for the common good of loving God and loving our neighbor in order to bring God the glory and praise due His name. We shouldn't live as spiritual orphans. We should commit ourselves to a people striving together to make that glory known to the watching world.

For one day, sooner than we all expect, Jesus will return to be with His people forever. It will be the perfect family reunion, without weird comments, veiled insults, disappointing absences or awkward moments. We will perfectly and wonderfully praise and glorify our Lord and Savior, Jesus Christ *together* (Revelation 5:10-13; 21:1-4). There will be perfect unity. When we gather as a family in local churches we proclaim that future hope by being united to local expressions of that spiritual family.

---

3   Revelation 7:9

4   Lister, J. Ryan, *Emblems of the Infinite King,* (Wheaton, IL: Crossway, 2019), p. 145

THE BODY OF CHRIST

Perhaps the best-known metaphor God uses to describe the church is that of a body. In the first chapter of Ephesians, Paul explodes with delight at the glorious redemption of those found in Christ. He declares the power of God in Christ, stating in verses 22-23: 'And he subjected everything under his feet and appointed him as head over everything for the church, which is his *body*, the fullness of the one who fills all things in every way.' (CSB) Christ is the head of the church, His very own body. This body image is useful for us to see the significance and importance of every member within God's body. Every member has a unique role and a part to play that is useful. Some are more obvious and seen, while others are more supportive and unseen, but all are needed and every one is valuable.[5]

Let's run with this metaphor for a bit here. Even without a basic biology class, we understand that a body won't work if you cut off its head. The head is the control-center, the starting point, of primary importance, which shows the necessity of Jesus being the head over all. This is not to say that He needs the church to be complete. He is complete in Himself. The image Paul uses is meant to show His supremacy in, and authority over, the church. He fills all things. Without Him we are empty. Without Him as our head we don't have a functioning body and we are, in effect, all just a bunch of amputated parts!

In 1 Corinthians, Paul addresses the congregation about proper, orderly worship in order to build up the faith of the weak and provide a more effective gospel witness to the non-believer. In chapter 12, Paul explains that the spiritual gifts God

---

5   For a more thorough treatment on this idea of the importance of unseen and quiet work in the local church see my article for 9Marks titled, *Secret Rewards of a Quiet Ministry,* https://www.9marks.org/article/the-sweet-rewards-of-a-quiet-ministry/

gives His people are *for the good of others*. He uses this image of a body stating, 'For just as the body is one and has many parts, and all the parts of that body, though many, are one body, so also is Christ' (v.12, CSB).

I studied kinesiology (exercise science) in college and it always amazed me how much time, money, and energy were regularly invested into researching peak performance in athletes. A body cannot function without its head, but as far as the other body parts go, a body can still function, somewhat, without all the parts in proper working order. But it will not function as efficiently or fully as it was designed. For optimal functioning every part must work. Every member of the body has a role to play! Even down to the unseen molecular level, if every cell isn't doing its job efficiently, it will have an impact on the athlete's performance. How much more with each individual member of a local church. Every member is of vital importance to the whole. Even '…the parts of the body that seem to be weaker are indispensable,' (1 Cor. 12:22). Nobody is superfluous. Every part impacts the whole. 'If one member suffers, all suffer together; if one member is honored, all rejoice together' (1 Cor. 12:26).

We are to steward the gifts we've been given for the greater good of the whole body. 'No member of the body exists to serve itself, nor does each member exist merely for its own private use. Rather, it puts its abilities to use for the other members of the body.' [6]

Our church building has an obscure set up. Without volunteers to help point people in the right direction, confusion would mostly ensue and what's worse, visitors might leave. What about lighting or sound? We need to be able to see and hear when we gather together. Imagine never having nursery workers or people to greet or hand

6   Calvin, John, *A Little Book on the Christian Life,* (Orlando, FL: Reformation Trust Publishing, 2017), p. 37

out bulletins. Praise God for the members who serve us in those ways. They are invaluable and often unseen.

Our unity as a whole is only possible because each unique part, though different, fits together as a complement to the other parts. The parts are not free-floating (like Thing in the Addams Family). Hands are not feet and eyes are not ears. Each has a different function, but works together with the others for the greater good of the whole. This unity is actually anchored in our differences.[7]

Diana loves people and enjoys being a part of the greeting ministry. Michael is quieter, but loves to serve on our security team making sure we are all safe while we gather. Caroline has been given an incredible voice from God and uses it with a group of musicians to help lead us each week in congregational singing. The beauty of God's design for His church is how the unity is highlighted by the respective parts working together in their diverse roles and with their diverse gifts. There is a unity in our diversity and a diversity in our unity. [8] Paul reminds the church at Corinth that, 'God arranged the members in the body, each one of them, as he chose.'[9]

Following his argument for unity in diversity from chapter 12 into the famous love chapter, 13, we see Paul is grounding this unity in the gift of love, which never ends. This is the seedbed for how we pursue our individual gifts as a body of believers. In 14:26, there is an understanding that they are gathering together for corporate worship when he says, '*When* you come together, each one has a hymn, a lesson, a revelation, a tongue or an interpretation. Let all things be done for building up.' Once again we see his thrust to encourage unity together as a local church. The gospel doesn't just create individual Christians. 'It creates a community, a family,

---

7   Horton, Michael, *The Christian Faith: A Systematic Theology for Pilgrims on the way,* (Grand Rapids, MI: Zondervan, 2011) p. 737.

8   Culver, Robert Duncan, *Systematic Theology: Biblical & Historical*, (Rossshire, UK: Christian Focus Publications, 2005) p. 873

9   1 Corinthians 12:18

a body. The gospel is church-shaped.'[10] A lone Christian is just that, alone. And being alone doesn't show the whole picture. It can't.

THE BRIDE OF CHRIST

My parents love each other passionately and deeply, and I've always marveled at how they do it. Fifty-two years married and if you asked them they'd tell you they wouldn't change a thing, except for maybe just a little more time together. They've known better times as well as worse; seasons of poverty and seasons of wealth. They've weathered the storms of sickness and basked in the sun of good health. And they most certainly love and cherish one another all these years later. When so many married couples don't seem to make it, couples like my parents, beckon us to look at their lives and ask, 'How? How did they do it after all those years?'

When we see an older couple walking together, hand in hand, we think, 'I hope that's us someday.' There's something alluring about true love stories that span the years. Young love is sweet, but mature love is powerful. The raw commitment and perseverance it takes to stick it out year after year and still have such tender affection for one another is captivating. We are drawn to these stories because as image bearers of God Himself, we were created to be a part of the best love story ever told. The love story of Christ for His church!

The Bible begins and ends with a marriage ceremony. However, what is being communicated is more than just romantic love. It's bigger than just two weddings. God is giving us a visual image of His commitment and love for His people and for His glory. Right out of the gate, in Genesis 1:26-28, we read about God uniting Adam to Eve as one flesh, commanding them to be fruitful and multiply, filling the earth with His likeness. In the last book of the Bible, Revelation 19:6-9, we read of the beautiful ceremony of the marriage supper of the Lamb. The Lord God is uniting Himself

---

10   Leeman, Jonathan, *Doctrine of Church Lectures*

fully, finally, and forever to His bride,[11] His people,[12] the church. They are the radiance of His glory. They are people from every tribe, tongue, and nation[13] dressed in His robes of righteousness, washed white in the blood of the Lamb. God is binding Himself to His people, His treasure, His dwelling place to manifest His glory to the whole earth. It's the ultimate love story of all love stories: God's love for His people for the sake of His own glory and fame. As Christians, we are grafted into God's redemptive storyline of history.[14]

I don't know about you, but when I attend a wedding and the door opens for the bride to come down the aisle, I may quickly glance at her, but my eyes dart directly to the groom. Why? Because the look on his face communicates adoration, longing, desire, deep love. The day they have waited for is here and they are going to become one. As the church, we are the bride of Christ and we are loved with an everlasting love by our Savior that is more powerful than any look from a groom at the end of an aisle. In Ephesians 5 Paul tells us we, as His church, are sanctified by Christ, washed clean by the Word of God, 'so that he might present *the church* to himself in splendor, without spot or wrinkle or any such thing, that she might be holy and without blemish' (v. 27). He does the choosing, the washing, the preparing, the presenting so we can be brought before Him one day as that radiant bride.

The marriage of Christ to His bride, the church will be fully, finally, and forever consummated at the end of all time. Now is a 'foretaste of glory divine,'[15] for those whose lives have been hidden in Christ. This life acts more like a rehearsal dinner. For

---

11   Ephesians 5:32

12   1 Peter 2:9

13   Revelation 7:9-10

14   Romans 11:17

15   Crosby, Fanny; 1873 hymn, 'Blessed Assurance', v. 1

the Christian at the end of time, there will be a celebration like no other and that celebration will have no end. On that day, our faith will become sight as we, His church, behold His unveiled face in full glory.[16] It's the very best love story ever told. And it's true!

THE DWELLING PLACE OF GOD

One of the glorious realities of the new covenant is the gift of God's Holy Spirit. The Spirit has been present from the very beginning. Genesis 1:2 tells us that, 'the Spirit of God was hovering over the face of the waters.' God's presence was with His people in the wilderness as a pillar of smoke by day and fire by night (Exod. 13:21). In Exodus 19 God's presence appears before His people at the base of Mt. Sinai. The people could not come to God, so God had to come to them. In Exodus 40:34, after Moses and the Israelites completed the work on the tabernacle we read, 'Then the cloud covered the tent of meeting, and the glory of the LORD filled the tabernacle.' Desiring a permanent place for God to dwell, Solomon erected the temple. Upon completion a supernatural event occurred again, 'As soon as Solomon finished his prayer, fire came down from heaven and consumed the burnt offering and the sacrifices and the glory of the LORD filled the temple' (2 Chron. 7:1).

For the Israelites, the hope was that God's presence would remain with them in this temple Solomon built. But the sinful hearts of the people would lead them into idolatry and abandonment of the God they professed to love and worship, thus defiling the temple. 2 Chronicles 36:15-16 says, 'The LORD, the God of their fathers, sent persistently to them by his messengers, because he had compassion on his people and on his dwelling place. But they kept mocking the messengers of God, despising his words and scoffing at his prophets, until the wrath of the LORD rose against his people, until there was no remedy.' God's anger burned against His

16   Revelation 22:4, 9

people and He vowed to destroy it all. 2 Kings 25 tells the horror of this destruction and captivity of God's people. But God kept the covenant He had made with His people and had compassion on them. When they returned from exile they would reconstruct a new temple, though the temple would never be what it once was under the reign of Solomon. (You can read of the men weeping at the sight of the newly constructed temple that was nothing like the first in Ezra 3:12-13.) The longing for a better, more perfect temple, burned in the people's hearts. The prophets regularly spoke of a restored temple for God Himself to dwell with His people.

When the New Testament opens, we read John the Baptist's prophecy, 'he who is mightier than I is coming, the strap of whose sandals I am not worthy to untie. He will baptize you with the Holy Spirit and fire' (Luke 3:16). The spirit was to baptize them? What did that mean? The people listening would not understand that prophecy until after Jesus had been raised from the dead. Upon completion of Jesus' earthly mission, the purpose of the temple was no more. The Great High Priest, Jesus, entered into the Holy of Holies, heaven itself, on our behalf, making the ultimate and final sacrifice for sins with His own body. He is not only the fulfillment or the replacement of the temple (John 1:14-18; 2:19-22), He is God Himself. Theologian Edmund Clowney states, 'God's true dwelling is not a tent of goatskins, or a temple of cedar and gold, but the flesh of Immanuel.'[17] Symbolizing the end of the separation between God and man, the curtain separating the Holy of Holies in the temple was torn in two, opening the way for us to God's presence by Jesus' own blood.

In the beginning of Acts, Luke tells us the resurrected Jesus' last words to His disciples, 'And while staying with them he [Jesus] ordered them not to depart from Jerusalem, but to wait for the promise of the Father, which, he said, "you heard from me; for John baptized with water, but you will be baptized with the Holy Spirit

---

17 Clowney, Edmund, *The Church*, (Downers Grove, IL: IVP, 1995), p. 45

not many days from now"' (Acts 1:4-5). But it wasn't until the day Pentecost arrived, another supernatural event, that the Spirit was poured out on His people to indwell them.[18] The second chapter of Acts describes it this way, 'When the day of Pentecost arrived, they were all together in one place. And suddenly there came from heaven a sound like a mighty rushing wind, and it filled the entire house where they were sitting. And divided tongues as of fire appeared to them and rested on each one of them. And they were all filled with the Holy Spirit and began to speak in other tongues as the Spirit gave them utterance.' God's spirit now resided *in* His people, not just individually, but corporately. Paul does refer to the bodies of individual Christians as temples. But the bigger picture is that God dwells in a special way in the local church as His temple (1 Cor. 3:16-17). God dwells with His people through His Word!

When we call the church a temple, this is in fact what the prophets foretold.[19] We are a kingdom of priests and God's presence is with us as His chosen ones, a holy nation, a people for His possession.[20] This is what Paul means when he writes of the church being a temple, 'in [Christ] being built together into a dwelling place for God by the Spirit.'[21] Notice we are being built *together* into a dwelling place for the Spirit. When we gather together the Spirit actively dwells in our midst. As Jesus said, 'For where two or three are gathered in my name, there am I among them' (Matt. 18:20). He was talking about His dwelling by the Spirit with the church.

CHURCH MEMBERSHIP: THE CEMENT

What do all these biblical images have to do with us today? If we are the body of Christ, the bride of Christ, the temple of Christ, a

---

18   Acts 2:4

19   G.K. Beale *The Temple and the Church's Mission*, NSBT (Downers Grove, IL: IVP and Leicester: Apollos, 2004), pp. 123-167

20   1 Peter 2:9

21   Ephesians 2:20-22

family, how does that intersect with our lives each and every day? Consider the commonalities of these images. They all share the idea of being connected, integrated, knowing and being known by others. The Bible's language for these images is corporate, not just individualistic because as I noted earlier we are the people of God, not just persons of God. These metaphors teach us about church membership because the *gospel creates a community of believers.*

I have to assume that if you've picked up this book to read you must wonder a little about the church. If you are a regular 'church goer,' have you ever asked yourself why you should bother to join the local church you're attending? For years now I've had friends and family tell me the idea of membership sounds constricting and institutionalized to them. They prefer meeting God in their own way and on their own time without having other people know all their business. They believe the Bible doesn't really have anything to say about church membership – we just need some fellowship with other believers. Maybe that's you. Or maybe you don't mind the idea of membership, so long as you get to mind your own business and other people do too. Or it could be that you feel perfectly comfortable being 'put on the roll' of the church, but don't really know what you're committing yourself to when you join? Do you know why it's important to be a member of a local church, and what it means?

Church membership is a specific commitment, a covenant, made between Christians. Believers unite themselves not because of any particular shared interests or similarities, but out of their mutual love and affection for Christ and the desire to make His glory known to the world. Members of a local church are joined together by the one Spirit of God with the express purposes of affirming one another's profession of faith by the means of the ordinances[22] and of spurring one another on in their discipleship to Christ. As we've seen, we Christians carry an individual witness,

---

22   See chapter 5 for more on ordinances

but *without the picture of the church we aren't telling the whole story*. The church is how the gospel is evidenced to the world; not just one lone Christian, but a people. It's a corporate witness. God has always been about a people! His people. You should join a church because, like the church, membership is God's idea!

Many Christians resist church membership for a variety of reasons. It's been suggested to me numerous times that if someone is a part of the universal church, there isn't a need for what they consider an official 'commitment' to the local church.[23] These people tell me all about their Bible study groups and Christian podcasts they listen to regularly, explaining how formal commitment to a local church isn't necessary. Other well-intentioned saints attend local churches week after week, getting involved in the work and ministry there without ever joining that body of believers in membership. It seems they don't join because they don't see any need.

Church membership is a part of God's plan to display the gospel by making disciples through our collective worship, work, and witness. I once heard it said that, 'If the Bible (The Word, Jesus Himself) is the cornerstone of the church, then membership is the cement that holds the congregation together.' I'm not an architect or engineer, but I do know you must have cement to hold bricks together.

THE EARLY CHURCH: MEMBERSHIP IN PRACTICE
We've seen how the Bible's images for the church lead us to church membership, but let's take a minute to see how church membership has been practiced. The word 'membership,' is not explicitly stated in Scripture, but the concept can be seen not only in the images used to describe God's people, but in the practices of the early church. Christians have always joined churches. This

---

23 In chapter 1 we discussed the difference between the local and the universal church.

isn't a new phenomenon. It's an historical practice with its roots in God's Word.

The book of Acts is of great help to us here. In Acts 1:15 there is a reference to the 120. This was the number necessary to form an official Jewish community with a new council.[24] It's here that we see a formal gathering of brothers and sisters begin as the Apostles and followers of the Lord Jesus assemble to wait together for the promised Holy Spirit to come.

After the Holy Spirit is poured out on the church in Jerusalem on the day of Pentecost, Peter preaches a sermon and about 'three thousand souls' were added to their number (Acts 2:41). These Christians 'devoted themselves to the apostles' teaching and the fellowship, to the breaking of bread and the prayers' (Acts 2:42). Acts tells us they 'were together and had all things in common...day by day, attending the temple together and breaking bread in their homes...praising God and having favor with all the people' (Acts 2:44-47). The result is at the end of verse 47, 'And the Lord added to their number day by day those who were being saved.' What a picture of worship, work, and witness!

As we continue through Acts, the gospel spreads and local congregations begin popping up around Asia Minor and the Middle East. It wasn't just singular men and women moving around sharing the good news of Jesus. It was men and women working together to share the gospel message and *establish churches* that would in turn make more disciples. This is why almost all of the New Testament was written to churches or church leaders, not individual Christians. And all of the books of the New Testament were intended to be circulated to local churches to be read for their edification.[25]

---

24 Marshall, I. H. *Acts: An Introduction and Commentary Vol. 5*, (Downers Grove, IL: IVP, 1980), p. 68

25 See Folmar, Keri, *The Good Portion: Scripture* (Ross-Shire, UK: Christian Focus Publications, 2017), chapter 4 on the circulation of books of the Bible and how it relates to the divine inspiration of Scripture.

Christians, indwelt by the Holy Spirit, established churches where the Word was sung, read, prayed, and taught (Acts 3:42-27). Care was given to know and be known by one another. Metrics of growth are noted throughout the book of Acts in words and phrases like, 'many,' 'increased in number,' and 'number of disciples.' They kept records, including lists of widows. This data suggests some kind of membership rolls. In Christopher Green's book, *The Message of the Church,* he helpfully states, 'Luke held together the eternal, invisible element of salvation with the temporal, visible element of church membership, which again can only be God's work: the Lord added to their number day by day those who were being saved.'[26] Salvation is indeed the work of the Lord, but manifested in the rolls of local churches.

From the beginning, Christians understood that *to be a Christian is to belong to a church*. The early church in Acts doesn't refer to random individual Christians living in the world, but a group of believers joined together for the express purpose of shining the gospel light to a lost and dying world. Christian and church are not the same thing, but they are related. Church is the plural of Christian that becomes singular in purpose. As Green explains, 'The church is people, but billions of Christians are not a church. 'Christians' and 'church' are not synonyms. For 'Christians' to become 'church' they must do something.'[27] They must commit to one another and to living out their corporate responsibilities together! Becoming a Christian is an individual act with corporate implications. You become a part of God's family and that becoming is reflected in a church's membership roll. It's only a half truth to say one belongs to the invisible, universal church if she does not belong to the visible local church.

---

26 Green, Christopher, *The Message of the Church*, (Downers Grove, IL: IVP, 2013), pp. 106-107; Acts 5:14

27 Ibid, p. 59

CHURCH AS OUR MOTHER

Christians committing themselves to local churches continued in the early centuries of the church, such that third century Christian leader Cyprian famously said, 'no one can claim to have God for his Father, and not have the church for his mother.' Local churches weren't social events in which to be seen, performances to be admired, or service providers you occasionally visited to get a tune up for the soul. They were the weekly means by which the Bible was taught, Christians were discipled, and God was making Himself known to the rulers and authorities in the heavenly places (Eph. 3:10).

Sadly, this biblical understanding slowly gave way to many unbiblical understandings between the fourth and sixteenth centuries. Grace, which had been rightly understood as a free gift of God's undeserved mercy, was taught as something we merit by our good works. The gospel was no longer the wonderful news of God reconciling a people to Himself though the blood of Jesus, but humanity cooperating with God to save themselves by their own blood, sweat and tears. The Church was seen not as a gathering of people but as a dispensary of God's grace for a price (indulgences).

Such abuses led many, like the German reformer Martin Luther or French reformer John Calvin, back to the Scriptures. These and other reformers argued that the Scriptures alone should dictate church doctrine and practice. They noted the marks of a true church as the right preaching of the Word (especially on sin and salvation) and the right administration of the ordinances, namely baptism and the Lord's Supper (and by extension church discipline).[28] These marks are upheld on a local level, not a universal one.

Since then a rejection of Scripture has led some to a liberal understanding of the church as a social center and human institution rather than a creation of God Himself. We can hear this in sermons that discount the resurrection of Christ and see it in 'ministries'

---

28   This will be developed more in chapters 4–6.

that focus on activities that help meet physical needs, neglecting the spiritual. Pragmatism has also stepped into the doors of the church replacing biblical convictions and a true understanding of the doctrine of the church. You can look around and see how the church has been affected by this today. We're tempted to judge a church by their parking, slick lighting, welcoming atmosphere, and how engaging the music is, as opposed to whether the gathering is filled with God's Word and prayer, and the sermon was theologically rich and biblically sound. And yet, even in this climate, the true church of God has continued, persevering and even thriving as she heralds the gospel truth as a witness to a lost and dying world. God has sustained her year after year by His will and His Word, as His people gather together in local congregations declaring His truth about our sinfulness and His mighty power to save. The household of God is truly 'the church of the *living God*, a pillar and buttress of the truth.'[29]

The church is *Christ's bride and body, the Father's family, and the Spirit's temple*. As believers we are united because of Christ's work on the cross for all those who turn from their sin and trust in Christ. But only together do we fully display His triune deity to the watching world. As Jonathan Leeman has said, 'Once you choose Christ, you must choose his people, too. It's a package deal. Choose the Father and the Son and you have to choose the whole family, which you do *through* a local church.'[30]

PASSPORTS OF THE HEAVENLY KINGDOM

In the summer between my junior and senior years of college I traveled overseas to study history with some of my fellow college students. One of the vital parts to traveling without our parents meant we needed to be in charge of all our important things, like

---

29 1 Timothy 3:15

30 Leeman, Jonathan; *Church Membership* (part of 9Marks Building Healthy Churches Series), p. 11

our passports! Passports are those legal documents that formally declare our citizenship. Losing a passport was not a small problem. Our professors made sure we were being responsible with them because if lost, functionally there would be no way to immediately validate our claim to be American. We would have to go to an American embassy and a diplomat under the authority of the ambassador would have to do the research to find out if we were, in fact, citizens of the United States.

As God's chosen people, in-dwelt by His Holy Spirit, 'our citizenship is in heaven, and from it we await a Savior, the Lord Jesus Christ...'[31] As citizens of heaven, life on earth is actually one of exile. We are living in a foreign land, awaiting the return of our King to bring us our forever home. Therefore, our local churches act as embassies in a foreign land with the members' citizenship in heaven. An embassy is a body of persons entrusted with a sovereign mission to represent the interests of their kingdom in a foreign land. We refer to these citizens as ambassadors. They are often on temporary assignment or mission from their government to accomplish specific tasks. So we could say as the church acts like an embassy, so her members are ambassadors. We have been tasked by God to make disciples and represent His name together, as a body of believers in our local churches. Paul says as much in 2 Corinthians 5:20, 'Therefore, we are ambassadors for Christ, God making his appeal through us.'

Embassies don't actually make people citizens of their country. They simply declare who is, and who isn't, a citizen. A true citizen carries a passport authenticating the holder's identity and native country. As churches, we represent the interests of heaven here on earth. When someone claims to be a follower of Jesus, the church does not make them a citizen. The church simply stamps their passport, affirming their claim or discards it, declaring it a fake. This

---

31   Philippians 3:20

is what it means to have the keys of the kingdom.[32] As an embassy in a foreign nation promotes the welfare of its citizens in that country and shows what the culture is like; it also protects the homeland by denying entry to those who are not citizens of that state.

If you aren't a member of a local church then you aren't fulfilling your job responsibilities as an ambassador for the King of Kings. True citizens of heaven demonstrate their citizenship by submitting themselves to the local church, an outpost of God's heavenly kingdom. It's there where we confirm one another's claim to belong to Jesus as we worship, work and witness together to build up and make more disciples of the Lord and King. *Church membership is an endorsement of a person's claim to be a Christian.* Our local church 'passports' protect our witness as well as promote God's glory in our lives as we live them out together.[33]

The keys we hold as ambassadors protect the kingdom's message. The keys were given not only to the leaders of local churches but the church as a whole. Protecting the gospel is not just for staff and elders. It is a job for the whole church. Jonathan Leeman states, 'the work of protecting and promoting the gospel and gospel ministry does not belong to the professionals; it belongs to the whole church.'[34] This is why it's so important to join your local church: you have a responsibility to know fellow members' lives and the message they profess.

The Privilege

GRASPING HANDS

One of the privileges of joining a church is how we can practically and tangibly encourage our brothers and sisters in Christ on their

---

32   See discussion on Matt. 16:19 in chapter 1.

33   Leeman, Jonathan, *Doctrine of Church* Lectures

34   Leeman, Jonathan, *Don't Fire Your Church Members,* (Nashville, TN: B&H Publishing, 2016) p. 121

journey to heaven. When we speak gospel truths to one another and demonstrate faithful living, our strength can help carry another member along in a season of struggle or doubt. But the reciprocal is also true. When we become a member of a church we are, 'grasping hands with each other to know and be known by each other. We are agreeing to echo and encourage each other when we need to be reminded of God's word in our lives or when we need to be challenged about major discrepancies between our talk and our walk.'[35] God tells us in Ephesians 2:10 that 'we are his workmanship, created in Christ Jesus for good works, which God prepared beforehand, that we should walk in them.' Part of those good works is spurring one another on towards 'love and good deeds...not neglecting to gather together with one another.. but encouraging one another,'[36] for we are 'built together into a dwelling place for God by the Spirit.'[37] We promote one another's holiness as we dig into each other's lives, helping one another follow Jesus.

The old adage is true, we are better together. God's good design shows that, 'Two are better than one, because they have a good reward for their toil. For if they fall, one will lift up his fellow. But woe to him who is alone when he falls and has not another to lift him up!'[38] By His good design, we're stronger as a team and we accomplish more when we work together. These ideas all stem from God's blueprint for us as a church body. We are meant to encourage other believers in their faith and relationship with Christ. We were created to work together as covenant people of God, in worship of Him. When we become Christians 'our identity shifts from 'me' to 'we.' We are trained to consider others more important than ourselves (Phil. 2:3-4). Our hearts fall in love with seeing God glorified in someone else as much as when He is glorified in our own lives.

---

35 Dever, Mark, *Why Join a Church*, (Wheaton, IL: Crossway, 2004) p. 39-40

36 Hebrews 10:24-25

37 Ephesians 2:20

38 Ecclesiastes 4:9-10

Some days we wake up and sigh from the reality that a new day has begun and we are just not ready to face it. Other days we delight to hear the birds singing and praise God for His goodness to us in so many ways. Both of those extremes have their home in the local church. It's there that we can pull a struggling brother or sister up when they are down or let them pull us up when we are down. When we link arms we have the support to keep walking forward in faith. It allows us to invest in each other's lives and work together to grow up to full spiritual maturity. It acts as a safeguard for one another as we face these schemes of the devil.

Throughout Scripture we read about the battle we are in as believers in the Lord Jesus. Ephesians 6 rings true to us as we try to wrap our minds around this unseen spiritual war going on all about us and combat the fiery arrows of the evil one. Like soldiers in a battle we are each facing enemies individually, but also as a group. A line from the U.S. Army Ranger Creed says, 'I will never leave a fallen comrade to fall into the hands of the enemy. Under no circumstances will I ever embarrass my country.' That sounds like the members of a local church!

He who started the good work in us is faithful and He promises to complete it.[39] And one of these means of grace in our growth is the body of believers, the local church. Discipleship within the church involves both the individual and the group. It is an individual project as we follow Christ and a corporate activity as we help each other along the way.[40] The church is God's vehicle for His own glory, but it's also the place He has provided for us to thrive. You should join a church for both yourself and for others. J.C. Ryle helpfully stated, 'Much of our spiritual prosperity depends, under God, on the manner in which we employ our Sundays.'[41]

39   Philippians 1:6

40   Mark Dever, *Why Join a Church?*, p. 34

41   Ryle, J.C. *Expository Thoughts on the Gospel of Luke: A Commentary,* (Angelo Press, 2020), p. 110

So initiate! Set up that group you so badly want to be a part of! Reach out instead of waiting for someone to reach out to you. I guarantee you aren't the only lonely or anxious member of your church. One of Satan's biggest ploys is to get individual members of a church body separated from others, to feel as though no one else can relate or cares about them. Individualism and the idol of self kill the beauty God has designed for His bride, the church in the corporate display of His glory to the world.

The 'Team Jesus' Jersey

In 2004 actor Kurt Russell starred in a movie as the new head coach of the U.S. men's olympic hockey team. The individual players all had exceptional skill and unique aptitude, but struggled to gel together as a team. The Olympics were fast approaching. Russell, in a moment of frustration and fury, prods them with these words: 'When you pull on that jersey, you represent yourself and your teammates, and the name on the front is a lot more important than the one on the back.' For those of you unfamiliar with these jerseys, the team name is on the front and the player's personal name is on the back. So in effect, the coach was saying, your individual contribution is important, but not nearly as important as your corporate one!

So too with the local church. When you commit to your local church, you put the 'Team Jesus' jersey on. You are, in effect, telling the world, '*I'm* with them and *we* are for Jesus.' This is as it should be, because biblical pictures and historical practices of the church tell us that the gospel creates a community of believers committed to one another. So what will you do? If you are a Christian, put the jersey on and join your little spark together in a roaring fire of collective heat.

QUESTIONS

'A ROARING FIRE: THE IMPORTANCE AND PRIVILEGE OF CHURCH MEMBERSHIP'

As God's chosen people we were created by God for His glory, and He has purpose for our lives individually and collectively. As a Christian, you are cemented as a brick into His house, uniting you not only to Christ as the cornerstone, but to His people, all the other bricks of His house. The local church is the embassy where we declare His truths in a foreign land, promoting and protecting His interests here on earth as we await His certain return.

1. What do the New Testament metaphors for the church have in common?

2. Read Galatians 3:27–4:7. What does our reconciliation with God mean for our relationships with other believers?

3. What is something you can do this week to give care, show love, or express gratitude to another brother or sister in Christ in your church?

4. Just like a body missing a part, so the church also needs every person to exercise his or her gifts for the edification of the whole. How might you better serve the body of Christ in either seen or unseen ways? How will that affect our unity?

5. Name one aspect of being the bride of Christ that excites and encourages you and tell why.

6. Read 1 Corinthians 3:5-17. If your life is built together with Christ and His people, then how should that affect your everyday living?

7. How is church membership implied in the biblical images we considered?

8. How can we think about the role of the church in the world today and what she is to represent? How might church membership play a role in that?

9. What should you do if you don't find a church that fits what you're looking for?

10. Have you ever considered that the best way to evangelize is to join a local Church? Why might that be?

11. If you haven't joined a local church, why not?

Part 2

What Does the Church Look Like?

Chapter 4

A Devotion to the Word:
Preaching, Teaching, Reading, Singing, Praying

Speak, O Lord, as we come to You
To receive the food of Your Holy Word.
Take Your truth, plant it deep in us;
Shape and fashion us in Your likeness,
That the light of Christ might be seen today
In our acts of love and our deeds of faith.
Speak, O Lord, and fulfill in us
All Your purposes for Your glory.

'Speak, O Lord'
Keith & Kristyn Getty

Cooking and baking are two very different things. Cooking allows for some degree of latitude and permits one to improvise, even experiment. Baking, on the other hand, requires precision and order. So when you're cooking and accidentally add the salt before the potatoes, you don't ruin the dish. Not so with baking. Add the eggs and the flour together all at once, and you can ruin the entire cake. Both baking and cooking do require specific ingredients and directions. You can't make chicken soup without chicken, or, heaven-forbid, chocolate chip cookies without chocolate chips! The ingredients matter, but the way they are combined matters with some dishes more than others.

God has given us the ingredients for, and the directions on, how He is to be worshipped in the weekly gathering of His people. He is the head chef! The writer of Hebrews warns us saying, 'let us offer to God acceptable worship, with reverence and awe, for our God is a consuming fire' (Heb. 12:28b-29). The ingredients for worship do not change, but how they are mixed together (whether we're allowed latitude and freedom, or must exercise precision) matters in some areas more than others. What are those areas? How do we think through those areas of the church's life where we have freedom, and where we may not?

The Primary Ingredient

In part 2 of this book we're going to dig a little deeper into how the church should function as it is structured according to God's Word. What does a biblical church look like? Part 2 is more the diet of a healthy church, and the way those ingredients fit together to keep the spiritual bodies of the corporate life of God's people in good health. Here in chapter 4, we'll consider the fundamental and primary ingredient for the church: the Word of God.

When the early church gathered, they kept the Word front and center, devoting themselves to the apostle's teaching (Acts 2:42). They gathered together as the people of God to listen to the Word being read and preached (Acts 20:27; 1 Tim. 4:13; 2 Tim. 4:2;), to sing the Word together (Col. 3:16), to pray the Word (Acts 2:42; 1 Tim. 2:8;), and to encourage one another with the Word (Acts 2:42). This is no different for the church today. Not only are we to read, preach, pray, and sing God's Word, but we should also *see* the gospel in the 'visible words'[1] of baptism and the Lord's Supper.

---

1   Attributed to Augustine

Churches practice this Word-centeredness through the *right preaching of the Word*, *the right administration of the ordinances*, and *church discipline*. The right preaching of the Word is preaching that orients itself around, and grounds itself in, the Word of God. We will refer to this as *expositional preaching*. Expositional preaching is preaching where the main point of the passage is the main point of the message, applied to the hearts of the hearer. This kind of preaching is preaching in service of the Word as opposed to the agenda or opinion of the preacher.[2] The weekly gathering of God's people should have laser-like focus on God's Word. Not only should the sermons be centered on Scripture, but the prayers and singing also. This Word-centeredness should mark the whole of our gathered time together. In fact, God's Word should act as the focal point of all preaching and teaching in the church.

As the people of God, we are to be people of His Word. In the book of Acts the Bereans were praised as those who 'received the word with all eagerness, examining the Scriptures daily to see if these things were so' (Acts 17:11). We should model ourselves after these brothers and sisters, seeking to know and understand the Word of God. If you ever happen to be in the position of looking for a church family, the single most important thing to consider is whether or not the Word of God is preached regularly and cherished in all aspects of the church's life together.

Dry Bones Brought to Life

We have a God who speaks. He uses words. He creates by His Word. Throughout the entirety of Scripture we see the power of the Word of God and the resounding theme is that *God's Word creates God's people*. At the very beginning in Genesis 1, God speaks creation into existence. His words brought the breath of life to all living creatures, including man and woman. In Genesis 12 we read how God *called* Abraham out of Ur of the Chaldeans. Abraham heard the

---

2   Dever, Mark, *Nine Marks of a Healthy Church*, (Crossway, 2004) p. 40

words of God and responded by following God out of his country to the land of Canaan. In Exodus 3:4, we read of God calling out to Moses from a burning bush. There is wonder at the miracle of a burning bush not being consumed by the flames, but what is an even greater wonder is that God spoke audibly and directly to Moses through that bush. The words that God gave to Moses weren't only for him, but for the whole nation of Israel. He gave His Word to His people through this mediator, Moses, calling them out of slavery in Egypt as His own treasured people. In Exodus 20, God gives His law, His 'words,' to His people and by accepting His law they became His people.

In the story of the valley of dry bones in Ezekiel 37 we have a marvelous display of how life comes through the hearing of God's Word. It is His words that hold the power of life. The spirit of God brings Ezekiel out into a valley of many 'very dry' bones and is commanded by God to prophesy to them saying:

> O dry bones, hear the word of the LORD. Thus says the Lord God to these bones: Behold, I will cause breath to enter you, and you shall live. And I will lay sinews upon you, and you will cause flesh to come upon you, and cover you with skin, and put breath in you, and you shall live, and you shall know that I am the LORD. (Ezek. 37:4-6)

Ezekiel obeys God's command and preaches to these dry bones and watches as they begin to rattle and come together bone to bone, with sinews and skin! But these newly formed bodies had no breath in them, so God commands Ezekiel to prophesy to the breath and tell the breath to come on these bones. And again, Ezekiel obeys saying, 'So I prophesied as he commanded me, and the breath came into them, and they lived and stood on their feet, an exceedingly great army' (v. 10).

What a sight that must have been for Ezekiel to watch a valley of dry bones become a valley of an exceedingly great army! God then interprets this vision for Ezekiel explaining that the bones are the house of Israel, His people. He speaks a promise to them saying, 'I will open your graves and raise you from your graves, O my people....I will put my Spirit within you, and you will live' (Ezek. 37:12, 14).

I once heard about a preaching professor who required his students in preparation for their sermons to walk into the heart of a cemetery littered with headstones, and preach to the dead bodies lying in the graves. What a task! Using the image from Ezekiel 37, he gave these aspiring pastors a visual aid for their future occupation. It was to be a reminder to them that every time they fill a pulpit and preach, there will be some who are spiritually dead in the pews. They might be breathing oxygen, but their hearts are stone and not flesh (Ezek. 36:26). Only God can bring them to life through His Word. New life does not come by means of a clever story, fun diagrams, pictures on a screen. It does not come through _our_ ingenuity and creativity, but through the power of God's Spirit through _His_ Word.

So many of Jesus' physical healings were connected to the physical senses. As Jesus spoke, the deaf were made to hear, the blind were made to see, the dead were brought back to life. These healings are a physical picture of what happens when God's Word encounters our lives. He opens up our ears to 'hear' His call, 'see' the truth of who He is and who we are, and He brings us from death to life. God is in the business of bringing dead things to life *for the sake of His own name* (see Ezek. 36:22).

God's Word alone is what brings the dead to life, draws corpses from graves, puts breath into lungs, and implants His own Spirit into the hearts of His people. Jesus demonstrates this very connection of His Word to restoring, healing, and giving life. When Jesus spoke, His words were always obeyed. Theologian, Herman Bavinck notes about Jesus, 'It is always a word of God, this is, never just a sound, but a power, not mere information but also an accomplishment of his will, Isa. 55:11, Rom. 4:17, 2 Cor. 4:6, Heb 1:3, 11:3. By this word Jesus quiets the sea, Mk. 4:38, heals the sick, Mt. 8:16, casts out demons, 9:6, raises the dead, Luke 7:14, 8:54, John 5:25, 28; 11:43, etc.'[3] Nature obeyed; sickness obeyed; spiritual forces of darkness obeyed; even death obeyed. John 1:1 tells us that, 'In the beginning was the Word, and the Word was with God, and the Word *was* God' (emphasis mine). On the mount of transfiguration God the Father speaks as Jesus stands in glory, saying, 'This is my beloved Son; listen to him' (Mark 9:7). The writer of Hebrews opens with these words, 'Long ago, at many times and in many ways, God spoke to our fathers by the prophets, but in these last days he has spoken to us by his Son' (Heb. 1-2a). Jesus' words hold authority and power because He is the very Word of God.

God created His people by His Word and brings them to life through His Word. Thus His people continue to live 'by every word that comes from the mouth of God' (Deut. 8:3; Matt. 4:4). This truth is so central that Jesus Himself quotes the passage to Satan when tempted in the wilderness. Jesus had fasted for forty days and nights and was hungry when Satan suggested that He show He was the Son of God by commanding stones to become loaves of bread. Jesus responded: 'It is written, "Man shall not live by bread alone, but by every word that comes from the mouth of God"' (Matt. 4:4). If Jesus used the Word of God for sustenance, how much more do we need it?

Why would we make anything other than God's Word the central part of our gathered worship of Him? *The right preaching of the Word is the main ingredient of the church.* It's the core, the central part of God's people because it makes God's people truly *His* people. 'The very word *ekklesia* has its Old Testament background in the gathering of the people of God at Sinai to hear God's spoken

---

3   Bavinck, Herman, *Reformed Dogmatics, vol. 4, Holy Spirit, Church, & the New Creation* ed. John Bolt; trans. John Vriend; (Grand Rapids, MI: Baker Academic, 2008), p. 449.

word.'[4] When God first gathered His people to worship Him on the mountain, He used His Word to give them identity as His people. So today God gathers His church and gives them identity by His Word. God's Word creates a people and makes a people for Himself.

You Feed Them

When we moved to Arkansas we decided it would be good for me to head back to work part time as a hospital nurse. I had had the privilege of being home full time with my kids for eight years, so I felt a little nervous going back after so long. As a labor nurse, I knew how babies were born, but I didn't know this hospital, the staff and the nurses. It took six weeks of orientation until I felt like I knew my job responsibilities and my role as an RN in this labor unit. This doesn't always happen with jobs. Sometimes we don't get a clear job description. Motherhood certainly feels that way for me, especially with teen and young adult children. I often find myself praying God gives me direction on what to do for my kids. But Jesus isn't like that.

Jesus knew His role, His purpose for coming to earth. Jesus clearly knew His job responsibilities. He didn't apologize or skirt around the issue. He clearly communicated His priority to preach the good news. A few times in Jesus' ministry He escaped early in the morning to pray. One particular time when His disciples were overwhelmed by the crowds and the various needs pressing in around them, Peter exclaimed to Jesus, 'everyone is looking for you!' The disciples and the crowds were all looking for Jesus to perform more miracles, more healings, more visually stunning displays of His power. They had real, legitimate physical needs they wanted Jesus to meet! What's worth noting in this story is how Jesus responds. When confronted with these performance pressures, Jesus simply states His primary purpose in coming to

4   Clowney, Edmund, *The Church*, (Downers Grove, IL: IVP, 1995)

earth, saying: 'Let us go on to the next towns, that I may preach there also, for *that is why I came out*' (Mark 1:38, emphasis mine).

Now this is not to say Jesus did not care or was not concerned for these people's physical suffering. I believe this story is here to highlight Jesus' greatest concern: mankind's spiritual suffering. Jesus' obedience to His Father's will to preach the gospel, intentionally removing Himself from the crowds and all the physical needs around Him displayed His singular focus on the Word-centeredness of His ministry. He had come to seek and save the lost by preaching to a dead and dying world. The Word made flesh had come to live, die, and rise so that His people might be given the breath of life and live eternally with Him. The healing He came to give wasn't just a temporary reprieve from their physical suffering here on earth, but an eternal healing that spans all of time. Paul tells us in Ephesians 5:25-26 that, 'Christ loved the church and gave himself up for her, that he might sanctify her, having cleansed her by the washing of water *with the word*' (emphasis mine). Jesus came to heal souls eternally, not just bodies temporarily.

During His ministry on earth, Jesus gathered His disciples around Him, preparing and training them. In the miracle of feeding the 5,000 Jesus tells the disciples to give the people something to eat (Luke 9:13). The disciples were no doubt confused, trying to make sense of how they would possibly feed that many people. They verbally protest, but stick around to see what Jesus is going to do this time. He takes the five loaves and two fish, breaks them, and then gives the food to His disciples to distribute. Jesus not only fed the 5,000, He used the incident as a parable to teach. 'By giving the feast to the disciples to distribute, Jesus anticipates their unique ministry of transmitting the Word of God. They would feed His sheep (John 21:17). With the authority of Christ Himself, the apostolic band would pass on what they had received as the Word of God.'[5] This Word is the food for the church. Jesus' last words to His

---

5   Folmar, Keri, *The Good Portion: Scripture*, p. 57

disciples were piercingly clear on this point. He commanded them to go and make disciples. How are they to make disciples? They were to teach them to obey *all* that He had commanded them. They were to follow and obey the Word.

Devoted to the Word

The book of Acts is a record of the apostles' activities following Jesus' ascension to heaven. They begin their work making disciples, establishing churches. The apostles were the men specifically set aside and called by God to preach the good news of Jesus and all He had done and taught. The single focus in all their endeavors is the Word of God and making His gospel message known. The book reads as much like a collection of sermons as it does a record of activities. From the outset, the Old Testament and the testimony of Jesus are central in all they do and say. Peter even addresses the crowd following the flurry of Pentecost with a sermon from Joel 2 to explain that the promised Holy Spirit had come (Acts 2:16). So the apostles preach and call people to repentance and faith, gathering the people of God as they go – the first churches.

Those early churches devoted themselves to the apostles' teaching. The apostles traveled and taught, and the new churches soaked up their teaching.[6] The pattern we see in Scripture is people gathered around the Word.[7] That is what the church does. This is why Paul, in his letter to Timothy, the young pastor of the church of Ephesus, implores him to 'devote yourself to the public reading of Scripture, to exhortation (preaching), to teaching' (1 Tim. 4:13) and urges him to, 'preach the word; be ready in season and out of season; reprove, rebuke, and exhort, with complete patience and teaching' (2 Tim. 4:2). It is why he tells Titus to appoint elders who

---

6   For examples see Stephen's speech in Acts 7 and the disciples listening to Paul until midnight in Acts 20.

7   Green, Christopher, *The Message of the Church*, (Nottingham, UK: IVP, 2013) p.78

'hold firm to the trustworthy word as taught, so that [they] may be able to give instruction in sound doctrine' (Titus 1:9). The church gathers around God's Word. Like the apostles and their disciples, preachers today are to be devoted to the Word of God. Pastors are called to preach God's Word. They are to preach faithful sermons that do not say something new, but simply re-reveal the truth of God's Word week after week. As Christians we need to regularly hear that truth proclaimed with boldness and clarity to fasten the belt of truth around our waists as we combat the schemes of the devil and his lies.

The apostle Paul understood this acutely as a former blasphemer of God's truth. False teaching corrodes the soul. In his second letter to Timothy, Paul strongly and simply states, 'preach the word' (2 Tim. 4:2). The Ephesian church was plagued by false teaching. Paul knew the greatest weapon against this false teaching was God's Word. He tells Titus to 'teach what accords with sound doctrine' (Titus 2:1). It is no different for the church today. God has given the church the task of guarding this good deposit (2 Tim. 1:14). Pastors must preach it. Charles Spurgeon once said to his seminary students, 'We are not responsible to God for the souls that are saved, but we are responsible for the Gospel that is preached, and for the way in which we preach it.'

KEEPING THE MELODY CLEAR

When my children were very small I came upon some resources highlighting the benefits of reading aloud to children. Knowing my own love for books I eagerly began the practice, and am still reading out loud to my kids today (less frequently, of course, given the craziness of their schedules). Even as older teens and young adults, they still love it when I read to them. Why? I'd argue it's because we can all understand and personally identify with a story. Mankind has been telling stories since the beginning of time. Jesus spoke in stories called parables. He used them to communicate truths to those who would 'hear.'

The whole Bible is one large story about God told through multiple smaller stories, poems and teaching. It's somewhat like the baseline melody of a symphony with various other sounds harmonizing with it. The baseline melody sounds forth the eternal truth about who God is and what He has done. The harmonies highlight and accent that baseline melody. The entirety of Scripture is telling the story of God's purpose in history to bring about glory for Himself in the saving of His treasured people.

As we have seen this far, it is through the truth of God's Word that He creates newness of life. In Romans 10:14 Paul asks the rhetorical question, 'And how are they to hear without someone preaching?' He grounds his answer in God's Word saying, 'Faith comes from hearing, and hearing through the word of Christ' (Rom. 10:17). The main role of any pastor is to preach the Word of God. But it is possible to preach God's Word and miss the point!

It sounds like dissonance when the preached Word leaves out the melody of God's redemptive storyline in Scripture. Sadly, some well-intentioned preachers teach from God's Word, but their words miss the point of that text. They do not undergird their words with the overarching truth of God's revelation of Himself throughout the WHOLE Bible. They divorced their text from the rest of the story; the biblical theology of their passage was missing. What is biblical theology? Pastor Michael Lawrence defines it this way: 'Biblical Theology is the attempt to tell the whole story of the whole Bible as Christian Scripture.'[8] If biblical theology is the sum of the parts, then these misinformed pastors preached only the parts, missing the sum of it all.

---

8   https://www.crossway.org/articles/3-ways-to-define-biblical-theology/ See also: Lawrence, Michael; *Biblical Theology in the Life of the Church: A Guide for Ministry* (Wheaton, IL: Crossway, 2010).

The subtitle for the children's book, *The Jesus Storybook Bible,* puts it succinctly and clearly stating, 'Every story whispers his name.' As preachers and teachers of God's Word, the melody of God's plan for history in Christ Jesus should be ever present when preaching and teaching. As listeners we should have our ears open to ensure what we are hearing from pulpits is in line with that melody. Every word that proceeds from the mouth of God has a point and a purpose fitting in with God's redemptive storyline of creating and redeeming a people through Christ for His glory.

KEEPING THE GOSPEL CLEAR

Thinking back to our cooking lesson earlier in the chapter, I wonder if you considered why one bothers to cook? Do we usually cook to just look at the food, make a walk by in the kitchen at some point during the day just to see how everything is going? No! We cook so we can eat what we've prepared. When I am cooking brownies, none of my kids asks, 'Oh mom, can I just look at those?' No! Instead, with wistful eyes, they beg me, 'Pleeeeeease Mom, may I have a brownie?' Food prepared is meant to be eaten. God's Word preached is meant to be consumed. The Word of God is the central ingredient to our life together because it's what properly nourishes us and gives us life. It feeds us because it contains the hope of the gospel message.

The Old Testament points to the law and humanity's inability to keep that law. The message of the New Testament hones in on Jesus, the perfect law keeper who has come, making a way for sinners to be reconciled to a holy God. Every word of Scripture exists to expose and reveal these truths. As Louis Berkhof states, 'The law seeks to awaken in the heart of a man contrition on account of sin, while the gospel aims at the awakening of saving faith in Jesus Christ.'[9] The law and the gospel are needed. Faithful preachers of

---

9   Berkhof, Louis, *Systematic Theology* (Edinburgh: Banner of Truth Trust, 1958), p. 612

the Word know we must see our sin before we can repent of it and be reconciled to a holy God.

In John 6:35 Jesus says, 'I am the bread of life; whoever comes to me shall not hunger, and whoever believes in me shall never thirst.' It is only through the life, death, and resurrection of Jesus that any of us has eternal life through God's Word. This is why *the gospel message must be present in preaching.* If every story whispers Jesus' name, then the gospel message is always present in every passage. The book of Acts is filled with sermons because the apostles understood the importance of being Word-centered, focusing on the gospel message taught to them by Jesus Himself. They understood that the gospel is the Word of God that brings life. When Paul has a vision of a Macedonian man calling him to come and help them, he concludes, 'God had called us to preach the gospel to them' (Acts 16:10).

But what is the gospel message? It's the most glorious news of all time! The gospel is the good news of Jesus. At the beginning, God created and set His love on Adam and Eve. But they rebelled against Him, running after things that would never satisfy, destroying their relationships with Him and one another. Since then every human being in history has sinned. The wages of sin is death. But God, in unfathomable mercy, sent His Son, Jesus, to the earth in poverty and destitution to live a perfect life and then to face a horrific death on the cross to pay for the sins of all of those who would repent and believe in the Lord Jesus. But it doesn't end there. God showed His power over sin and death by raising Jesus from the dead, forever securing His people to Himself: those people who recognize their sin, turn from it and run to Him for newness of life. God's people are those who, by the grace of God alone, recognize their need for forgiveness and come to Him to receive His mercy.[10]

---

10 If you are not familiar with this gospel message, please find someone to talk to today about what it means to repent of your sins and trust in Jesus for reconciliation and to become part of His family, the church.

It's not an easy road. When we identify ourselves with Jesus we enter into a life of suffering as He did. Jesus said, 'If anyone would come after me, let him deny himself and take up his cross and follow me' (Mark 8:34). The cost may be high, but the payoff of eternal life with Jesus is so worth it!

This gospel message is what the Christian life is all about. It is the message that reconciles us to God, keeps us in His love and reconciles us to one another as well. So preachers must preach it clearly each week from the text of Scripture, for the benefit of unbelievers to hear and be saved and for the church to be built up together.

DWELL DEEP

If true expositional preaching isn't a part of your regular Bible diet, ask yourself why. Would you rather listen to topical sermons where passages are often forced to say what we want them to say? If that's the case, we risk hearing from man, and not from God. Good advice pales in comparison to God's power through His Word. We all enjoy encouraging and uplifting messages. But not everything in life belongs on a coffee mug. It's neither honest nor Christian to shy away from the hard stuff. Nor should we neglect topics that we deem unpalatable and unpopular. Is it our place to edit God's Word? To effectively 'cut out' the hard stuff, as Thomas Jefferson so famously did? We don't want 'fugitive preachers' who run away from the text, but faithful pastors who reveal the text. J.I. Packer has encouraged Christians to 'dig deep and dwell deep.' It is in the depths where the message of God's Word comes more alive as we

---

For when we become Christians, we are given a new family with our new hearts. The gospel not only reconciles us to God, but to His people as well. Also read Natalie Brand, *The Good Portion: Salvation*, for a full explanation of what it means to be saved and how God has secured salvation for His people through Christ.

see things that we might otherwise have missed by only raking the leaves off the top.

True expositional preaching preaches the *whole* counsel of God's Word and does not shy away from any of it. Paul claims in Acts 20:27, 'For I did not shrink from declaring to you the whole counsel of God.' Whether preaching Song of Solomon, 1 Corinthians 7, the census in the beginning chapters of Numbers, or the land allotments in Joshua, every word of these passages has proceeded from the very mouth of God and contains purpose and power. Expositional preaching is done in the service of our Creator and not finally in service of our present culture.

Reverberation

Word-centeredness should mark not only the preaching, but the entirety of the gathered worship service. As believers, we come together to hear the Word preached, but also to sing and pray the Word and see it displayed through baptism and the Lord's Supper (see chapter 5) 'The preacher opens his mouth and utters a word, God's Word. But the Word doesn't sound just once. It echoes or reverberates. It reverberates through the church's music and prayers.'[11]

Jesus referred to the temple as a house of prayer (Matt. 21:13). How much more should the church where God dwells with His people by the Holy Spirit be a place of prayer. We see this pattern in the early church. In Acts 2, they 'devoted themselves' to prayer (v. 42). In Acts 4, they pray for boldness and the Holy Spirit responds by filling them with boldness and shaking the place where they were gathered together (vv. 23-31). Jesus even gave the church a model in the Lord's prayer.[12] In the same way, singing was an integral part of their corporate worship. Paul encouraged the church in Ephesus

11   Leeman, Jonathan, *Reverberation: How God's Word Brings Light, Freedom, and Action to His People* (Chicago, IL: Moody Publishing, 2011), p. 25

12   Matthew 6:9-13

to address 'one another in psalms and hymns and spiritual songs, singing and making melody to the Lord with your heart' (Eph. 5:19). Similarly, he addresses the church of Colossae, 'Let the word of Christ dwell in you richly, teaching and admonishing one another in all wisdom, singing psalms and hymns and spiritual songs with thankfulness in your hearts to God' (Col. 3:16).

Singing and praying were, and are, integral parts to the gathering of God's people. We are to be singing and praying to God together in our churches today. But as Paul exhorted the Colossians, it should be the 'word of Christ' that dwells in us as we do so. Our singing and our prayers must be Word-centered. As carefully as God's Word is handled in the preaching, so too with the prayers and singing of the Word. What we sing and what we pray must be focused on the truth of God as revealed to us by His very own words.

SINGING TO THE LORD AND TO ONE ANOTHER

Whether or not we have drums or cymbals, amplified sound or a capella, the main ingredient of the singing of God's people must be God's Word. It is worth noting here that the command in Ephesians 5 is to address 'one another' when we sing. We are to sing 'to the Lord' but also to one another. If we cannot hear one another at all, how can we sing to one another? The command presumes that we can actually hear and be encouraged as we sing to one another. Choirs can make beautiful music, but we do not gather to watch other people sing. We need to open our mouths in praise together. For some of us that might simply be a joyful noise rather than a beautiful sound but when our voices meld together the melody is pleasing to our Lord. When we gather we are God's people singing the truth of God's words *to* one another in praise of Him.

PRAYING THE WORD

Whether or not a prayer is scripted or extemporaneous, it must be reverent and in accord with God's Word. This means that prayers in the gathering should be focused on the priorities and patterns we see in the Bible. The Bible is filled with examples of all types of prayers: thanksgiving, lamentation, repentance and confession, praise, and supplication. Often the prayer list of a church is filled with requests for physical needs to be met, but is that what we see modeled in God's Word? There's nothing wrong with praying for someone's physical health, but Jesus' focus was on healing the spiritual sickness He saw in the hearts of the people. We are chock full of sin sickness. Yet sadly, too often we pray more for saved people to stay out of heaven, than lost people to be saved from hell. David prayed for healing and rescue, but he also regularly praised the Lord regardless of his circumstances. Do we do the same when we pray corporately? Do we pray God's priorities for His church?

No Excuses

When I first sat under faithful expositional preaching my heart melted hearing God's Word. Yet I was anxious. The sermons weren't conversational. They didn't have a lot of stories. There were no 'ten ways to find joy in my week' or other kinds of simple application I was accustomed to. They made me think. But they fed my soul in a way I hadn't previously experienced. I found my heart longing to be in the Word more and to better understand it for myself. I even started preparing to hear it preached by studying the passage myself the week before the sermon.

But something else happened during that time. When old friends came to visit, I felt the need to explain, almost apologize for it. Sadly, I knew how unfamiliar and strange it would be for some to spend that much time looking in their Bibles during the sermon. And since the pastor was preaching through books of the Bible, we covered all the topics, including, believe it or not, hell on Mother's Day! So much for the Hallmark calendar. Yet it turned out to be just what our weary hearts needed as moms – a message on God's mercy and perfect justice.

There is no need to apologize for faithful expositional preaching. Nor is there reason to apologize for the Bible being read or the deep, rich lyrics of gospel-centered songs or biblical prayers. Sometimes passages will be difficult or dark, tackling topics that will offend or feel out of step with the current culture. Sometimes hymns will have difficult words or themes that take work to understand. And sometimes our collective prayers will have an outward focus on churches, peoples and lands that we don't know. But God in His own Word has assured us that His Word is sufficient. It is living and active even today and is filled with all we need to live the lives He has given us as we grow in godliness. We can trust God's instruction for the church.

My husband is a faithful and excellent preacher of God's Word. He just finished preaching a series to us from the book of 1 Samuel. Rich with biblical history and theology, Brad led us through the chapters of God's Word as the Holy Spirit opened our eyes to see the marvelous things in His Word. We as a church were thriving and growing, marching our way through the text week after week. And yet, difficult and challenging topics were in front of us. Brad tackled the hard stuff. Witchcraft, betrayal, suicide: Brad helped us think about these things biblically without sensationalizing them, faithfully preaching the passage and bringing glory to God. We as a body of believers were able to grow in the fullness of our understanding of God's character through those challenging texts.

A number of members reached out to Brad thanking him for not passing over the hard passages. Are you like one of those members? Do you desire to learn from *all* of God's Word, even if the passage doesn't seem to make sense upon first read or correlate with the current circumstances in your own life?

The main and most essential ingredient for the church is the Word of God. Without God speaking to us we would be starving, desolate, and blind. God's Word can defend itself. We don't need to excuse it or be embarrassed by it. C.H Spurgeon has said, 'The

Word of God is like a lion. You don't have to defend a lion. All you have to do is let the lion loose, and the lion will defend itself.' Expositional preaching, with good biblical theology that contains the gospel message, gospel-rich singing, and biblical prayers lets that lion loose!

Praise be to God who has not forsaken us or left us without direction. For He has exalted above all things His name and His Word. (Ps. 138:2). May you find a fellowship of believers in a local church that prizes the glory of God's name and His Word above all else. If you currently reside in a church that prizes those things, give God praise for the gift you've been given in your local church. If you don't, you ought to ask why, and pray long and hard over what you ought to do about it.

QUESTIONS

'A DEVOTION TO THE WORD: PREACHING, TEACHING READING, SINGING, PRAYING'

God's Word provides us everything we need for life and for godliness. It's also the backbone for everything we do when we gather together as a church. The Word of God should be preached, taught, read, sung, and prayed in our church services.

1. Why should God's Word be the main ingredient of the church?

2. If the Word of God raises the dead to life, what kind of investment are you making each day into that Word and how do you prepare to get all you can out of the weekly sermon?

3. Why is expositional preaching so important?

4. Why is biblical theology important for sermons, and if the church is made up of those who already believe the gospel, why should the gospel still be made clear in sermons?

5. What does Word-centered singing look like, and why is it important? What does it mean to sing to one another and to the Lord?

6. How can Scripture inform our prayers when we come together?

7. Do you desire to learn from *all* of God's Word even if the passage doesn't seem to correlate with your life upon first read?

8. How can you better prepare your heart each week to hear, sing, read, and pray the Word with your local church?

Chapter 5

A Visible Picture of the Invisible:
Baptism and the Lord's Supper

There is a fountain filled with blood
Drawn from Immanuel's veins;
And sinners, plunged beneath that flood,
Lose all their guilty stains:
Lose all their guilty stains,
Lose all their guilty stains;
And sinners, plunged beneath that flood,
Lose all their guilty stains.

'There is a Fountain'
William Cowper

In the late spring of 1989 I had a conversation with a junior high friend. I had shared the gospel with him, given him a Bible, and we talked extensively about spiritual things. I was anxious to know where he was. What did he make of the Bible? What did he think about Jesus? After multiple probing questions like these (which really wasn't anything new coming from me) he simply smirked and said, 'Oh, I think I became a Christian a while ago.' I was astonished, elated, and honestly a little frustrated he hadn't said anything sooner.

Without skipping a beat I blurted out, 'Well, then you need to get baptized. It's your first act of obedience after confessing him as your Lord and Savior.' Let's just say my friend was none too pleased with this news. For he despised speaking in public, anything that would have the spotlight on him.

'Why?' he asked with concern.

Precociously and confidently I stated, 'Matthew 28 tells us we are to be baptized as believers in the name of the Father and of the Son and of the Holy Spirit.'

My thirteen-year-old self knew baptism followed confession and repentance, but I'm pretty certain I didn't have much to add beyond that point. I wasn't able to explain what baptism symbolizes, who should or shouldn't be baptized, how someone should be baptized, or how baptism acts as a 'front door' to church membership. All I knew was that I really wanted my friend, who had just made a profession of faith, to obey Jesus.

Maybe that's you. But do all the details matter? What if they were already 'baptized' before? Does it have to be done by a pastor? Can't we just baptize someone in a tub during a evangelistic rally and call it a day? Or what about the school sink after your friend told you she became a believer?

Similar questions arise when we think about the Lord's Supper. Should we bother with the details of who should take it, when they should take it, how they should take it? My husband and I took communion together, alone, during our wedding ceremony. We wanted our first act as a married couple to be centered on our union in Christ. That seems pretty God-centered and pure. Surely there's no harm in that, right? Let's hold that answer and first take a look at what God's Word has to say to us on these topics.

We see the early church's understanding of commitment to a local church through the practice of baptism and the Lord's Supper.

These two practices we call ordinances (or sacraments depending upon your church tradition) are intrinsically tied to a body of believers. Baptism is both a personal and a public declaration. The one being baptized is personally declaring herself united to Christ and that declaration is affirmed publicly by the church she is also being united to. The Lord's Supper is the ongoing declaration together of our unity in Christ. Baptism brings one into a family. The Lord's Supper makes that family one. These two ordinances of baptism and the Lord's Supper, as Bobby Jamison so helpfully states, 'draw a line around the church. They make it possible to point to something and say "church" rather than only pointing to many somethings and saying "Christians."'[1]

Ordinances act like a hinge between the invisible universal church and the visible local church. Baptism and the Lord's Supper may not be issues essential to one's salvation, but they aren't unnecessary for us to consider. In fact, when executed poorly or misunderstood they can deeply confuse and muddy the waters around the gospel message itself. As secondary doctrines they hold deep theological meaning and significance. They are two of the prongs that hold that gospel diamond in place. It's worth our time to consider these two ordinances. What are they? Who are they for? And when and how are they to be practiced? Last chapter we looked at the gift of God's Word and the call to preach, teach, pray, and sing it corporately as God's people. Now we begin our journey down ordinance lane, where the gospel is displayed in picture form. Consider with me how God's Word is *seen* visibly in the practices of baptism and the Lord's Supper.

Baptism: Picturing the gospel

We're a water loving family. All six of us have been competitive swimmers at some point in our lives. Even our dogs love the water!

---

1   Bobby Jamison, 'How the Lord's Supper Makes a Local Church', *9Marks Journal*, 04-28-2016

Moving to Arkansas has afforded us plenty of opportunities to swim, wade, and float in the amazing Buffalo National River. But suppose on one of our float trips down the river we are joined by some friends who aren't yet professing Christians. Then suppose we are given an incredible evangelistic opportunity to share the gospel and one of our friends makes a confession of faith. If baptism is an act of obedience, should we dunk them into the running river water in the name of the Trinity? Can they just immerse themselves? Is this what the Bible refers to when it speaks of baptism? If not, why not?

If you aren't sure how to answer those questions, let's start with a working definition for baptism. *Baptism is the act of immersing one in water as a public profession of faith in Christ and the church's public declaration of that faith, thereby uniting the believer to the church and marking him or her off from the world.* Let's break this definition down into three parts.

Before we start, you may have noticed that our definition of baptism above doesn't include sprinkling of children who are too young to believe and declare their faith. I want to acknowledge that there are Bible-believing Christians who believe that the local church includes believers and their infant children. Presbyterians, Anglicans and some Congregationalists believe in infant baptism – and many of these evangelical saints are my dear friends. They believe that baptism is a sign of God's covenant with His people and is based on the obedience of the parents rather than the faith of the one being baptized. I'll directly address this below because I see the biblical warrant for 'believer's baptism,' but at the same time I want to affirm my love for my paedobaptist brothers and sisters, and I want to acknowledge their desire to be obedient to the Scriptures.

First, baptism is an *individual's* public profession of faith in Christ. Baptism is where we go public for Jesus. It's our chance to declare to the world that we are followers of the Lord Jesus Christ and desire to serve and love Him with all of our heart, soul, mind, and strength. We don't go public by walking an aisle at church or raising our hand in a room full of closed eyes and bowed heads. Baptism is how we 'come out' to the world and go on record for Jesus. Christianity is personal but it's not private. Jesus wants followers everyone can see. We step out of the darkness and into the light when we go public at baptism.

When we come to faith in Christ there is an internal and an external response. Inwardly we repent and believe, but outwardly we confess and declare this change. 'For with the heart one believes and is justified, and with the mouth one confesses and is saved' (Romans 10:10). Baptism is the outward symbol of the inward reality of being united to Christ. As Romans 6:4 explains, 'We were buried therefore with him by baptism into death, in order that, just as Christ was raised from the dead by the glory of the Father, we too might walk in newness of life.' Symbolized by the very act of our bodies being lowered into the water and coming up from it, we picture the union we have within Christ in His death, burial, and resurrection. The immersion of our bodies in water also pictures the washing of our souls by His blood. Additionally, it is the mark of an ongoing reality. When we are baptized we make ourselves known as a Christ follower, declaring our faithful allegiance to Him and our intent of walking according to His ways for all our lives. Baptism is a sign of the new covenant we have in Christ. It is a visible picture of the gospel for all to see.

Secondly, baptism is a *church's* public declaration of an individual's profession of faith. Baptism is an act of the church, not just the individual. This is the part we often miss or misunderstand. Baptism involves two parties: the one getting baptized and the church, affirming that person's faith to be valid. Biblically, we do not baptize ourselves. There's simply no precedent for that in Scripture. Someone always does the baptizing. This may sound stifling and overly formal. I've heard friends or coworkers refer to baptism as a 'me and Jesus' kind of issue, but it's not. Let me illustrate.

I am a registered nurse. The work I do in the hospital requires certain qualifications and certifications. What if I showed up for a job interview and proclaimed to be a self-certified RN? Claiming the hours I've poured over TV shows like ER & Chicago Med, I declare to have learned everything I needed to know to take care of patients.

That would be ludicrous! A proper nursing license requires education and a board certified exam. No matter how much someone might claim to be an RN, they must provide verification from another party. In a job interview I may say I am a nurse, but my license is what verifies the validity of my statement. Does this seem like mere semantics or even an infringement on a personal issue? My guess is that you might not care a whole lot about RN verification until a self-proclaimed nurse who learned how to start an IV by watching YouTube, showed up in your hospital room!

So who has the authority and right to speak for Christ to declare a person's faith to be valid? We've seen that local churches represent Jesus here on earth. In things like baptism, membership, and discipline, the church speaks for heaven on earth. Back in chapter 1 we discussed the keys of the kingdom from Matthew 16 and 18. That 'binding and loosing' terminology is legal in nature. The church 'binds and looses' through the practice of the ordinances of baptism and the Lord's Supper. (The practices of church membership and discipline are closely tied to these ordinances.) This is what Jesus was teaching when He gave the church the 'keys of the kingdom' and said 'whatever you bind on earth shall be bound in heaven, and whatever you loose on earth shall be loosed in heaven' (Matt. 16:19). In baptism, the *church* says to the world, under Christ's authority, 'to the best of our knowledge, this one is a Christian.' The church, in effect, hands the individual the 'Team Jesus' jersey, when they publicly affirm that individual in baptism, calling the world to 'look and see the gospel pictured in baptism.'

Thirdly, baptism *unites the believer to the local church*, marking him or her off from the world. In the covenant God made with Abraham, circumcision was the sign that marked off God's people to be recognized as part of the Israelite community.[2] Jesus said that His death would usher in a new covenant (Luke 22:20). Baptism is a sign of the new covenant we have in Christ. In the new covenant, we are united to Christ and we are also united to the church. In Acts 2 the newly baptized believers weren't baptized into free agency. They were added to the church in Jerusalem (Acts 2:41). 'In baptism one steps out of the world and steps into the church.'[3] Baptism is in effect the entrance to a local church. Sure, anyone is welcome to come hear the preaching and see the body, but it's through baptism that one enters in formally aligning with a local body through Christ.

Ephesians 2 shows us that when we are reconciled to God we are also reconciled to His people, His household, the church. Verses 1-10 lay out salvation by grace through faith and then verse 11 starts with a 'therefore.' Gentiles had once been alienated from God's people, Israel, 'strangers to the covenants of promise, having no hope and without God in the world' (v. 12). But Christ not only made peace between God and man, but He also reconciled both Jews and Gentiles 'in one body through the cross, thereby killing the hostility' (v. 16). If we are in Christ, we are 'fellow citizens with the saints and members of the household of God' (v. 19), no matter the religious or ethnic background from which we come. So when we go forward in baptism we are not only showing we are joined to Christ, but to His people, particularly in the fellowship of a local church. When we make this profession of faith in Jesus as our Lord and Savior, turning from our sins and trusting in Him for

---

2   In this patriarchal society only males were marked off, representing the females in their families as well.

3   Jameson, Bobby

our salvation we walk through the front door and are welcomed into His family.

It's one thing to kick a ball around, but if you're not wearing the jersey, who do you actually play for? Is there anyone to vouch for your claim? You need a team! Your team can verify your claim to be a part of the team. And even more than that, they work alongside you for the common goal to win the prize! (1 Cor. 9:24-27). Baptism is when one puts on the 'Team Jesus' uniform. They've joined the team. They're now accountable to their team mates and their coaches who are all working together towards a common goal.

OBEDIENCE NOT SALVATION

As important as baptism is to a believer, it is *not* an act that saves you. We are not saved through our baptism, and it is not required to be saved. We are saved fully and finally when we repent and turn from our sins, placing our faith in Jesus as our Savior. The Bible never separates baptism from salvation (cf. Acts 2.38; 22.16), and yet it does distinguish between baptism and salvation. Baptism publicly expresses a past event, picturing outwardly what has occurred inwardly. It is an act of obedience by a new believer, but it is *not necessary for salvation*. The thief was converted on the cross next to Jesus and was never baptized. Yet, Jesus assured him he would be with Him in paradise that very day (Luke 23:39-43). Baptism doesn't create saving faith, it only testifies to that saving faith.

Just because it is not saving and is not necessary for salvation does not mean that it is unimportant. Baptism *isn't optional* for the believer. Baptism is a commandment from the Lord to every believer and not a tradition invented by the church. Jesus commissioned His disciples to 'make disciples of all nations, baptizing them in the name of the Father and of the Son and of the Holy Spirit (Matt. 28:19). And we see Peter in Acts 2 telling those who were 'cut to the heart' by the gospel message to 'repent and be baptized, every one of you in the name of Jesus Christ for the forgiveness of your sins' (Acts 2:37-38). First John reminds us that obedience to God is the litmus test of our love for Him (1 John 2:3-6). If we love Him, we will keep His commandment to go forward in baptism.

If you say you're unwilling to go public for Christ, you're simultaneously saying you're unwilling to follow Christ. Baptism is the first item on God's discipleship 'to-do' list. I've known many young believers who are nervous, even terrified to go forward publicly with baptism. The idea of people staring at them is to live their worst nightmare. If that is you, take heart, your Heavenly Father knows your anxiety and calls you to cast it upon Him (Ps. 55:22). Our faith is not meant to be private; personal, yes, but not private. Private faith will become a passing faith. It will wither up and die.[4] That is why we are to confess with our mouths Jesus as Lord *and* demonstrate that public confession through the obedience of baptism. By confessing your faith you will in fact strengthen your faith. Not only will it strengthen you, but also those around you as they hear and see Christ professed.

Others may be terrified because such public identification with Jesus will bring genuine social, familial, maybe even physical persecution. Yet Jesus demands our total allegiance. Not only does He demand it, He's worthy of it, and this is what we proclaim in baptism. Not that it saves us or is necessary for salvation, but baptism is obligatory for those who profess to follow Christ.

Birth or new birth: Who should be baptized?

I have a couple of friends who identify as vegans. They've given themselves that label and their eating habits attest it's true. Let's suppose *I* give that 'vegan' label to another friend, but every time we go to lunch she orders the beef au jus sandwich. No matter how much I want to use that label for her, it means nothing if *she* doesn't hold herself out to be vegan. Baptism is similar. We don't baptize

---

4   Jameson, Bobby, *Church Basics: Understanding Baptism* (B&H publishing; 2016), p. 19

those who themselves do not identify as Christians. So who should be baptized? Short answer: All who profess faith in Christ. Baptism is for believers, and *only* believers.

In the old covenant, Theologian and pastor, Christopher Green states, 'Circumcision stood for promises made, but baptism stands for promises kept; circumcision stood for true circumcision being needed, but baptism stands for the spiritual circumcision, having occurred; circumcision marked the waiting for the true heir, but baptism marks believers as true heirs in the heir who arrived.'[5] Circumcision united people together into an ethnic group, a nation. The new covenant people are united together in Christ. What makes the new covenant new and, in fact, better (Jer. 31:31-34), is that all people in the new covenant possess the Spirit (Ezek. 36:24-28; Rom. 2:28-29; Phil. 3:3; Col. 2:11). Baptism is a marker of *spiritual rebirth*. So whereas circumcision says to Israel, 'Make yourselves new!', baptism says to Christians, 'This one has been made new!'[6]

So what does this mean for my paedobaptist[7] brothers and sisters? I have numerous godly friends who are paedobaptists, whom I respect and admire deeply. They offer some strong biblical arguments to support their position and yet we come to different conclusions on this issue. As we wade into the waters of infants and baptism things can get pretty nuanced. I don't have the space here to present a thorough assessment of a covenantal view of infant baptism, but if you do want to investigate the topic more, I would encourage you to read the books noted below.[8]

---

5   Green, Christopher, *The Message of Church*, p. 58

6   Jamieson, *Understanding Baptism*, p. 34

7   Paedobaptism simply refers to the belief in, and practice of, baptizing infants.

8   J. Murray, *Christian Baptism* (Phillipsburg, NJ: P&R, 1980), p. 69; L. Berkhof, *Systematic Theology* (1941; reprint, Grand Rapids, MI: Eerdmans, 1982), p. 632; R. L. Reymond, *A New Systematic Theology of the*

SLOW IT DOWN?

When we look through the book of Acts we see that, normally, believers are baptized right after coming to faith. See Acts 2:38-41; 10:47-48; 16:14-15, 30-3 and 19:15. Baptism was so closely connected to one's profession of faith it became a shorthand way of announcing one's conversion. That said, there are some ways the church in Acts is dissimilar to the church today. In that time, Christianity was not only illegal, it was scandalous. To convert often meant new believers had to walk away from family, friends, livelihoods, and sometimes their very own lives! This was not a 'Christian' society in which they lived. Baptism wasn't something you just 'did.' These were first generation believers which meant there were no Christian traditions or cultural Christian norms yet established. There wasn't pressure to go along with what others were doing. In fact it was quite the opposite. To go public for Jesus often meant persecution and death.[9]

Today, particularly in the western hemisphere, we face a different set of challenges. It is important for us to briefly consider them as we need to practice some caution so we don't run the car of baptism into the ditch on either side of the road. In many parts of the United States cultural Christianity still exists. Because Christianity is affirmed and encouraged in this context, there can be an inadvertent rush towards baptism. Baptizing believers too soon can result in a person who shows initial excitement about Christ deceiving herself, and the local church affirming a faith that

---

Christian Faith (Nashville, TN: Thomas Nelson, 1998), p. 936. Ferguson, Everett, *Baptism in the Early Church: History, Theology, and Liturgy in the First Five Centuries* (Grand Rapids, MI: Eerdmans, 2009), pp. 856-7. See Jewett, Paul, *Infant Baptism & The Covenant of Grace* (Grand Rapids, MI: Eerdmans, 1978) and Wellum, Stephen, 'Baptism and the Relationship between the Covenants' in *Believer's Baptism*, ed. By Schreiner and Wright (Nashville, TN: B&H Academic, 2006).

9   Stephen was the first martyr for Jesus. See his story in Acts 7

is not really present. But we must also show caution for the ditch on the other side of the road. We can run the risk of discouraging a true believer by having them wait inordinately long when their confession of faith appears credible. There's obviously a problem on either side of the road and only you best know your cultural context, but in my experience the ditch of rushing too quickly seems to be more common and have the more dire and lasting consequences.

In our twenty plus years of ministry life I've heard many baptismal testimonies about various kinds of 'wet adventures' that took place prior to one's true conversion, only for the person to be truly saved later and come to be baptized in reality for the first time. Just this past month a dear friend of mine and I discussed this very thing! 'It's the strangest thing. I had been thinking about it a little, but it wasn't until I started reading all of these things about baptism that I realized I haven't actually been baptized. I got dunked as a kid, but that was before I ever made a true confession of faith in the Lord Jesus. I don't think my baptism was a genuine profession of trust in and submission to Christ.' This friend clearly understood she was saved years later and needed to be obedient to go forward in her public profession of faith. Baptizing too quickly or too young doesn't give people time to count the cost of following Christ and risks deceiving them into thinking they're genuinely Christians, when, in fact, they're not. Maybe they haven't taken the time to really understand what they say they believe or aren't willing to follow Christ when the going gets tough. [10]

ROLLING DOWN THE RIVER: THE MECHANICS OF BAPTISM

This brings us to our final consideration in baptism: How should a believer be baptized? First, and most importantly, a believer is to be

---

10   There are those who truly struggle with the assurance of their faith and whether or not their baptism is genuine. I encourage these women to seek the counsel and care of the elders in her church to work through those particulars.

baptized into a gospel-preaching church. The new covenant creates a people who can be seen by the world, the local church. Baptism is a picture of the one being brought into the fellowship with the many, a visible people of God. If the church holds the keys to the kingdom to declare the what and who of the gospel (see chapter 1), and baptism is a public profession of that gospel message, then it is the responsibility of the church to perform the baptism. If there isn't a gospel witness of a church to accompany the baptism, it's an empty, or worse, false sign to the world.

Now there are exceptions, as in the case of the Ethiopian Eunuch in Acts 8. It seems his conversion and subsequent baptism were in isolation from any gospel-preaching church. The Ethiopian believer had no church to go back to. He had to follow Christ alone for the time being. In essence, he was being sent back home as a missionary to his people. Yet, where there are gatherings of Christians in the New Testament, baptisms happen within those gatherings.[11]

If baptism is an act of the church, then who should perform the baptism? Should a close friend or a parent baptize? What about the person who originally shared the gospel with the one being baptized or the one who brought him or her to church? Since baptism is an ordinance of the church, with the church affirming the faith of the one baptized, the person performing the baptism should normally be someone who's been set apart with pastoral authority in the church. It doesn't need to be the head pastor, but it should be someone the church has recognized to lead and shepherd the flock, such as an elder or overseer (see 1 Tim. 3:1-7, 5:17). Although not biblically required (cf. 1 Cor. 1), if the church speaks for Jesus, it seems prudent that the baptizer is authorized to speak for the church. This would argue against friends or family members performing the baptism. Though not necessarily wrong, when parents baptize their children, it can appear more like a family celebration rather than an ordinance of the church.

---

11   Acts 2:41, 8:12, 10:48, 16:15, 16:33,

Second, baptism is to be done in the name of the Trinity as commanded by Jesus Himself. In Matthew 28:19, Jesus' departing words were a command for His disciples to go and make disciples, 'baptizing them in the name of the Father and of the Son and of the Holy Spirit.' Baptism is a public declaration of an individual, recognizing the three persons of the Trinity as the one true God to whom he or she is giving full allegiance.

Third, a baptism requires water. How much water is necessary to accomplish a proper baptism? Sprinkling, pouring, dunking, diving? A pool of water? Running water? The Greek word used in the Scriptures for baptize means 'to plunge' or 'immerse in water.'[12] This makes sense because full immersion in water best symbolizes the washing of the believer from their sin and their unity with Jesus in His death and resurrection (Rom. 6:3-5).

Let's go back to our hypothetical float trip down the beautiful Buffalo River. After reading through this section on baptism, how would you now feel if I pulled my canoe over with this new professing Christian and baptized her right then and there? Lord willing, you would respond in great joy to her profession, but encourage me to pause the baptism, and instead invite her along to church, knowing it was there where she could gather with God's people. They could get to know her and affirm her faith. She would then have the privilege to display the gospel publicly through her baptism, declaring to the world that she is united to Christ and His people.

The Lord's Supper: A family meal

I shared that my husband and I took communion together as our first act as a married couple. While our intentions and motives were honorable (desiring to focus on God first in our marriage and highlight that dependence upon Him before the family and friends

---

12 βαπτίζω in BDAG

who had gathered to witness the exchange of vows) we missed the point and meaning of the Lord's Supper. Let me explain.

The Lord's Supper was instituted by Jesus Himself. In Luke 22:14 we read:

> And when the hour came, he reclined at table, and the apostles with him. And he said to them, 'I have earnestly desired to eat this Passover with you before I suffer. For I tell you I will not eat it until it is fulfilled in the kingdom of God.' And he took a cup, and when he had given thanks he said, 'Take this, and divide it among yourselves. For I tell you that from now on I will not drink of the fruit of the vine until the kingdom of God comes.' And he took bread, and when he had given thanks, he broke it and gave it to them, saying, 'This is my body, which is given for you. Do this in remembrance of me.' And likewise the cup after they had eaten, saying, 'This cup that is poured out for you is the new covenant in my blood. But behold, the hand of him who betrays me is with me on the table. For the Son of Man goes as it has been determined, but woe to that man by whom he is betrayed!'

Jesus' final supper with His disciples was eaten on 'the day of Unleavened Bread on which the Passover lamb had to be sacrificed' (Luke 22:7). Considering the Passover helps us to better understand this New Testament supper. In Exodus we read the story of how the Egyptians 'ruthlessly made the people of Israel work as slaves and made their lives bitter with hard service, in mortar and brick, and in all kinds of work in the field. In all their work they ruthlessly made them work as slaves' (Exod. 1:13-14). But God was not unaware of their suffering. He said to Moses, 'I have surely seen the affliction of my people who are in Egypt and have heard their cry because of their taskmasters. I know their sufferings, and I have come down to deliver them out of the hand of the Egyptians' (Exod. 3:7-8a). And deliver them, He did! He gave the Israelites specific instructions for this special Passover meal which included unleavened bread and the blood of a lamb. God said to them, 'The blood shall be a sign for you, on the houses where you are. And when I see the blood, I will pass over you, and no plague will befall you to destroy you, when I strike the land of Egypt' (Exod. 12:13). He rescued them from their slavery and death through the blood of a sacrificial lamb. The Passover would define who God's people were, where they had come from, and what God did to save them. Year after year this glorious deliverance was commemorated with a meal. The people were to remember that they were saved not because they were deserving, but because they were covered by the blood of a sacrificial lamb.

Returning to Luke, Jesus is identifying Himself as the final Passover lamb, changing the meal from symbolizing deliverance from slavery to Egypt, not into deliverance from Rome or some superpower, but into deliverance from slavery to sin and death. God is transforming the Passover meal right before the disciples' eyes. This is why Jesus calls it the 'new covenant in my blood' in verse 20. For the old covenant, with all its laws, rules, regulations, and the sacrifice of animals, was powerless to effect heart change. But now God, because of 'the precious blood of Christ, like that of a lamb without blemish or spot' (1 Pet. 1:19) writes His law upon the heart of every Christian.[13] So the meal that had been celebrated in nuclear families within ethnic Israel becomes a celebration with Jesus and His disciples. No longer would it be a meal for biological family, but one for those who have faith in Christ. The people of God are redefined.

When we hear the word 'supper' we may think of a meal with people gathered around the table conversing with one another. It feels intimate and personal. But what about when we call it the 'Lord's Supper'? Is that a fancy way of talking about a church potluck? No! *The Lord's Supper is how a church communes with Christ and one another as they commemorate Christ's death, commit themselves*

---

13   Jeremiah 31:33, Hebrews 10:16

to one another, and anticipate His certain return. It is one of the two ordinances given by God to the church. Baptism and the Lord's Supper are visible displays God has established for us to 'see' the gospel, His redemptive work on our behalf. Some of you may be more familiar with the term 'communion.' This word simply refers to 'communing' with Christ and His people. It's simply a different word for the same ordinance.[14]

LOOKING BACK, LOOKING AROUND, LOOKING FORWARD

Jesus tells His disciples to 'do this in remembrance of me' (verse 19). The cross has historically been a symbol of Christianity. But, biblically, we remember Christ by the Lord's Supper, not by a cross hanging on the wall in our church building. The very first thing we are doing when we come together to partake of the Lord's Supper is to look back, remembering the past. We remember Christ's body broken for us. In 1 Corinthians 11, when Paul discusses the Lord's Supper, he repeats Jesus' words after both the breaking of the bread and pouring of the cup, 'Do this in remembrance of me' (vv. 24, 25). When we partake of the Lord's Supper we remember that Christ's body was broken and His blood was poured out as payment for the sins of His people. We not only remember Christ, we also remember our own past. We remember with repentant hearts the sins for which He has paid and from which we have been saved by His death and resurrection.

When we partake of the Lord's Supper we also look around, considering that Christ's body was broken for us, His people, to make us His body.[15] When we gather together as His people over this supper, we testify to the present reality of Christ's body, the church here on earth. In 1 Corinthians 10:16-17 Paul writes, 'The cup of blessing that we bless, is it not a participation in the blood

---

14 In the interest of simplicity and clarity I will be referring to 'the Lord's Supper' or 'communion' synonymously.

15 1 Corinthians 12:27, 1:23, Colossians 1:18

of Christ? The bread that we break, is it not a participation in the body of Christ? Because there is one bread, we who are many are one body, for we all partake of the one bread.' As we participate in the meal, we participate together in the benefits of Christ's death. We're reminded of His commitment to us, to never leave us nor forsake us (Deut. 31:6, Heb. 13:5). We're refreshed by the promise of the Spirit He's given us (John 14: 25-27). Our fellowship with Christ actually creates fellowship with one another. So when we remember His commitment to us, we look around and are reminded of our commitment to one another within our church. We are one, because we share in the one bread. 'Just as baptism binds one to many, so the Lord's supper binds many to one.'[16]

We can borrow a helpful picture from marriage to better illustrate. Though not a perfect analogy it may help our understanding. When two people are married each person makes vows and covenants to the other in front of witnesses. Baptism is like placing the ring on your spouse's finger at your wedding. You're telling the world, 'I'm in!' with the congregation there to witness and confirm that declaration. The Lord's Supper is like the ongoing exclusive intimacy in a marriage, which confirms a couple's vows to one another. But instead of two becoming one, as with marriage, it's more like many becoming one through the Lord's Supper as we proclaim our unity with Christ as His own body.

Finally, we look forward when we partake together of the Lord's Supper, proclaiming the future kingdom to come. Together we recall Jesus' promise to His people and anticipate the reality of His certain return. When we eat the 'bread and wine,' they don't literally transform into the body and blood of Christ, they symbolize it. The supper gives us a visible sign of His spiritual

---

16   Jamieson, Bobby, *Church Basics: Understanding the Lord's Supper* (Nashville, TN: B&H publishing; 2016); pp. 33, 36-40. For a more in-depth treatment of this statement, look at Dr. Jamieson's other work, *Going Public*, (Nashville, TN: B&H publishing, 2015), pp. 134-135.

presence with us. The Lord's Supper is so much more than some kind of divine post-it note reminder on our refrigerator. It's more than even some old faded picture of great days gone by. It's the anticipation of the best event of all eternity! Think of looking at the invitation to the most spectacular party you can imagine. As Jesus said, 'I will not drink [the wine] again until the kingdom of God comes.' (Luke 22:18) The table is a dress-rehearsal for that day when Jesus Himself will stand at the head of the banquet table. We will witness a feast unlike the world has ever seen. That's the hope we proclaim. A hope that energizes us daily in the skirmishes and battles of this fallen world. Every time we eat the bread and drink the cup we 'proclaim the Lord's death until he comes' (1 Cor. 11:26), awaiting that day of endless rejoicing.

THE INVITATION LIST

So if we are looking back, looking around and looking forward at this family meal, who should partake of the Lord's Supper? Anyone in attendance that day in the church building? How about children? What about my friend who's not sure she wants to follow Christ?

The Lord's Supper is a commemorative meal for baptized believers in the Lord Jesus Christ who are members in good standing of a local church.[17] First, that means it's for those who trust in Jesus' death to save them. It is not for the children of believers or extended family of believers. Nor is it an evangelistic tool for unbelievers to participate in. In a time when so many are concerned about excluding or not welcoming, this can be a challenging truth to comprehend. But in 1 Corinthians 10:21 Paul writes, 'You cannot drink the cup of the Lord and the cup of demons. You cannot partake of the table of the Lord and the table of demons.' Later on in chapter 11 verse 27 he writes, 'whoever eats the bread or drinks the cup of the Lord in an unworthy manner

---

17   Paedobaptist traditions require a profession of faith before taking the Lord's Supper.

will be guilty concerning the body and blood of the Lord.' Paul is explaining that God's table is exclusive! God requires us to come to Him on His terms, not our own. He will only have us through Christ and in Christ. The Lord's Supper does not save. It does not make you 'good with God.' Only Jesus can do that through His shed blood on the cross. The meal is for those whom God has reconciled to Himself, for those who have repented, declaring all out war on their sins, and fled by faith to Christ for refuge. God's table is set for His children. What rejoicing there should be when we believers gather together with the express purpose of reminding one another that the table has been set for us, His children?

Second, the Lord's Supper is for baptized believers. In Acts 2 we read of the new believers breaking bread (another way to refer to what we call the Lord's Supper) together *after* they had been baptized (vv. 41-42). Baptism is how we profess our initial faith in Christ, but the Lord's Supper is how we *renew* that faith and commitment to His body. As Christians, we must first make a confession before we can renew a confession. Baptism is one of the requirements to come to the Lord's table.

Third, the Lord's Supper is for church members. Some churches require membership in their church to partake of the Lord's Supper and others invite any in attendance who are members in good standing of a gospel preaching church. In either case, membership is necessary. In the New Testament there were no such things as 'churchless' Christians. The repetitive phrase in Acts, 'come together' referred to the gathering of God's people, a church. One must join a family before they sit down to the family table. *You can't sit for a family meal without a family*. If communing with Christ's body is the essence of the Lord's Supper, how can you commune with what you've never committed to? Communion is the sign of our inclusion into the family of God, sealing His promises to us as His children.

THE RECIPE

Communion is an ordinance God gave to the church. He did not give it to individual Christians or to the nuclear family, but to the spiritual family of God present in local churches. It is something the church does as a whole. It is an act of the church, not individual church members fractured from the body doing it on their own. In Pauls' letter to the Corinthian church, one of his main concerns for them was how the Lord's Supper was being administered. Paul, in great frustration over the wealthy in the church turning this corporate celebration into a private party, begins his comments with, 'For, in the first place, when you come together as a church...' (1 Cor. 11:18). Paul understands that the Lord's Supper is meant to be celebrated by the church, as a church. The refrain 'when you come together' is repeated four times in the passage (vv. 18, 20, 33, 34). Paul understood that communion was meant for all of the body, not subsets of the body. And the command to 'discern the body' (1 Cor. 11:29) presumes a quantifiable local church body is present.

When the ordinance is divorced from the local church, it loses its symbolism and meaning. Though not done intentionally, all those practices that remove communion from the local church undermine the very unity the Supper is meant to promote! It isn't a mystical or personal kind of experience with God that we enjoy on our own, closing our eyes to shut out the rest of the church. Nor is it the appropriate symbol for a bride and groom to show their commitment to the Lord. It's not meant for stirring up emotions at Christian conferences and camps. It's even out of place at hospital beds. So when we took communion at our wedding our intentions were honorable, but we were inadvertently undermining the very thing God intended to picture – the unity of His gathered assembly in Jesus Christ.

Exactly how the elements are distributed will vary from church to church. I suggest the preferable practice is to have the congregation remain seated while the Supper is distributed. This best captures the corporate nature of the family meal which the Supper is meant to represent. When we sit and pass the elements, we replicate the experience of sitting together around a table, passing the food from one hand to the next. Though it's not wrong to come forward, that practice has historically been associated with the Roman Catholic Church where one must approach the altar and receive grace through the mediation of a priest. And coming forward and taking individually can minimize the corporate nature of the Supper being celebrated *together*.

As we gather week by week, how often should we take the Lord's Supper? Should we take it each time we gather? Once a month or quarterly? As per the Lord's command, His Supper should be a regular fixture of the church, like teaching, fellowship and prayer (Acts 2:42), but the New Testament doesn't clearly prescribe what regularly means. Acts 20:7 says, 'On the first day of the week, when we were gathered together to break bread…' This may suggest a weekly celebration. However, 1 Corinthians 11:25 says, 'as often as you drink it,' suggesting some degree of flexibility.

Those who practice it weekly believe it's important to provide the body of believers this means of grace during every gathering. Conversely, those who practice it less frequently (monthly, quarterly, annually) fear that a more frequent practice could lead to callousness, causing the Lord's Supper to become nothing but a rote formality. But there is grace for us in these decisions about frequency. We need to get the motivation right. The motivation for the Lord's Supper should be for the people of God to gather often to remember, reflect, and anticipate the work of the cross of Christ.

Along with the right motivations, the Lord's Supper should be taken with a spirit of preparation and self-examination. 1 Corinthians 11:28, 'Let a person examine himself, then, and so eat of the bread and drink of the cup.' No matter the frequency of the ordinance, introspection and remembrance of our life in Christ must be a part of the preparation. If the Supper is not practiced weekly, it's helpful for a church to give its members at least one week's notice for them to prepare their hearts. During this time of reflection we should be asking ourselves probing questions: How am I walking with others in Christian love? Am I rejoicing with them in joys, bearing their burdens and sorrows? Am I living above reproach in the world, avoiding harmful gossip and excessive anger? Is there any uncontested sin in my life or in the lives of others in the body? We are remembering our commitment not only to Christ but to one another.

We can also prepare ourselves by reminding ourselves why this Supper is even necessary. We remember Christ's death on our behalf. We were in desperate need of forgiveness and salvation from ourselves and our sin. We remember what we have been rescued from by His bodily sacrifice for us. He gave His life for us. We also remember what we have been rescued for – an eternal life with Him in perfect glory. The reality of the cross of Christ should cause our hearts to come to His table with reverence and honor, but also with great joy. For we have been made alive in Christ!

Is this how you approach the table? Do you come with a mix of wonder and rejoicing? Do you look around the room at the brothers and sisters you've committed yourself to and praise God for uniting His people through the cross of Christ? Do you rejoice around the table of your King knowing He is coming back to bring His people home where we will feast with Him in heaven?

THE STORY IS STILL GOING

Thirty-one years later I am now married to that junior high friend I implored to be baptized. God's grace is all over that story (but that's another book for another time). Suffice it to say, that young boy who was afraid to step on stage before the church to confess his allegiance to God now steps into the pulpit week after week preaching the good news of Jesus Christ to the world. He also leads

God's people in the ordinances of baptism and the Lord's Supper. He has the unique privilege of holding out these beautiful pictures that display God's merciful love for His chosen people.

God began a good work many years ago in our lives just as He has in the life of every believer. What's even more exciting is the truth of His faithfulness and the reality that He promises to complete the work He began, working until the day of Christ Jesus (Phil. 1:6). So as we wait with our brothers and sisters, declaring God's goodness in the lives of those going forward in baptism, bringing them into our family, the local church, and breaking bread together, we drink of that cup proclaiming the Lord's death together until He comes. And we cry, 'Come, Lord Jesus, come quickly!'

QUESTIONS

'A VISIBLE PICTURE OF THE INVISIBLE: BAPTISM AND THE LORD'S SUPPER'

God gave His church two ordinances that display the gospel both individually and corporately. Baptism symbolizes our identification with Jesus in His life, death, and resurrection while the Lord's Supper commemorates Jesus' death and our corporate identification as the people of God.

1. How do the ordinances act like a hinge between the invisible universal church and visible local church?

2. What does baptism symbolize?

3. Who is baptism for? And when should someone be baptized?

4. What is required for baptism?

5. What is the Lord's Supper, and who is it for?

6. What does the Lord's Supper symbolize?

7. What are the three directions we should 'look' when taking communion?

8. Who should be participating in communion? Should we encourage our children to take it with us? Why or why not?

9. What things can you do to prepare yourself for the next time your church has communion?

Chapter 6

A Pursuit of Holiness:
Church Unity and Discipline

How rich a treasure we possess, in Jesus Christ our Lord
His blood our ransom and defense His glory our reward
The sum of all created things are worthless in compare
For our inheritance is Him whose praise angels declare
How free and costly was the love, displayed upon the cross
While we were dead in untold sin the Sovereign purchased us
The will of God the Father demonstrated through the Son
The Spirit seals the greatest work the work which Christ has done.

'How Rich a Treasure We Possess'
Matt Boswell

Discipline. What do you think of when you read that word? What comes to mind? Sports training? Practicing an instrument? Raising children? This idea of discipline carries varied connotations, many of which are negative. Images of military reform schools, cruel taskmasters, and even abuse come to our minds. Discipline is often contrasted with love. Because of these associations, many parents today struggle to even utter the word 'No' to children because it can feel restrictive and harsh. Parents want the best for their children, and it can be hard to see when we're exchanging temporary peace for potential long-term chaos. Christian parents want their children to grow, develop and thrive, and ultimately confess Christ as Lord. The Bible tells us to 'bring them up in the discipline and instruction of the Lord' (Eph. 6:4). We can struggle to surround them with the safe training hedge of correction. And of course I speak as a mom! It was hard to keep moving forward in faithful correction and discipline of my children. Even when it was apparent they were running headlong into sin without any regard for my warnings, I wanted to bury my head in the sand of blissful ignorance, exhausted from the task I faced, feeling unsuccessful and worn out.

Unfinished projects

As Christians, we know we are incomplete, unfinished projects. We recognize we have been called out of darkness into the marvelous light of Christ, and yet we still wrestle with our sin. Paul tells the church at Philippi how grateful he is for them and their partnership in the gospel, but he also reminds them of their need for God to do more work in their lives. He writes, 'I am sure of this, that he who began a good work in you will bring it to completion at the day of Jesus Christ' (Phil. 1:6). Paul says that he's not already perfect, but he presses on (Phil. 3:12). We occasionally need the correction or admonition of a cautious friend. Proverbs 27:6 tells us 'faithful are the wounds of a friend; profuse are the kisses of an enemy.' Deep down inside of us we know we're not perfect people, which is why correction becomes a necessary part of how we grow. True discipline isn't retributive punishment. True discipline's goal is improvement and growth.

Discipline comes in two forms, formative and corrective. Formative discipline comes in what we typically consider more 'positive' forms. It's like the stake next to a tree to help it grow tall and straight. It's the encouragement from a coach on how to improve your game or the advice of an older mother you talk with as your kids play in the playground. Formative discipline in the church looks like the teaching we receive in Sunday school class or sermons. It's the exhortation and instruction we get from books and conversations with friends. It shapes and steers us towards holiness and godliness. The vast majority of discipline seen in the Bible is this positive form. It's discipline that's meant to train and develop us – to make us more like Jesus.

Corrective discipline is what we consider the more 'negative' form. It might look like a parent with a child who has disobeyed, a teacher assigning detention for missing homework, or a coach making an athlete run laps after practice for goofing around. More seriously it could be a judge sentencing someone to prison for criminal conduct. In the church, it might look like admonishment from a pastor or friend to someone flirting with sin. it could be a rebuke by the elders or even rise to the level of formal excommunication.

Though we think of such discipline as 'negative,' even corrective discipline has a positive aim. The overarching goal is not to punish, but to restore one to fellowship with Christ and His body, the church. Both formative and corrective discipline have a good place in keeping the church a unified, shining light in the world.

Declaring war on our sin

The problem we face in churches today is that most of us don't think of discipline as a loving kindness. Church discipline sounds judgmental, legalistic, and punitive. We say things to ourselves and others like, 'Isn't God about unconditional love? If we start going around judging everybody, we'll become graceless, heartless, loveless people. We'll become that gross caricature of Nathaniel Hawthorne's Puritan New England. What next, the Salem witch trials? How could church discipline possibly serve the cause of the gospel?'

Maybe that's how you feel. Maybe you opened this book right to this chapter wondering how someone could ever explain church discipline in a way that isn't self-righteous and judgmental. My prayer is that those who read this chapter would actually be encouraged to uphold the purity of the church for the sake of God's name through the practice of church discipline.

As with many things in Christianity, there has been plenty of confusion and misinformation about church discipline; and sometimes there has been genuine abuse. Practiced rightly, though, church discipline is one of the best ways to love our brothers and sisters in Christ as we protect the purity of the church and maintain her gospel witness. If we avoid church discipline, we are in effect claiming that we know how to love people better than God does. His Word tells us that He 'disciplines those he loves' (Heb. 12:1).

I think one of the struggles we face in understanding and accepting this notion of proper church discipline is actually a struggle to fully grasp the gospel. There are two different 'versions' of the gospel preached in evangelical churches today. One stresses the simplicity and ease of believing; you get a ticket to heaven and unconditional love without demands. It's decision-focused and belief-centered. It presents Jesus as Savior for our really bad sins, but not as Lord over the whole of our lives. Many things are missing from this version, most especially the terrifying holiness of God and total depravity of man. God is the one who brings men to Himself by setting His unmerited favor upon them.[1] Another thing missing is *cost*. Jesus spoke clearly and deliberately about the cost of following Him: 'If anyone would come after me, let him deny himself and take up his cross and follow me' (Mark 8:34). We in no way earn our salvation, we love Jesus above all and therefore are obedient to Him! For He prepared good works in advance for us to

---

1   Romans 5:6-11, See J.I. Packer's discussion of the old and new gospel in the introduction to John Owen's, *The Death of Death in the Death of Christ*

do.[2] The works do not save, but they are the necessary byproduct of the one who has been saved.

The second, and I would argue the true version of the gospel, focuses on the King to whom we owe everything. When we see this God before us, a God who chose to set His love upon us, gave His Son for us, and will keep us until the very end,[3] there is a demand for holiness. This gospel has a call to be and make faithful disciples. It's not just some decision to make. It's repentance and faith![4] It presents Jesus not just as Savior, but also as Lord. If a church is built around a gospel that confesses little, demands little and requires little, church discipline won't make any sense. Yet Christ Himself taught that every branch that does not bear fruit will be cut off (John 15:2). We are called to bear fruit in keeping with repentance (Matt. 3:8).

Jesus doesn't just give us a new status when we are saved. He gives us a new nature (live differently), a new family (the church), and a new job description (holiness).[5] If our gospel doesn't communicate this, it's not the gospel. Coming to Christ doesn't mean you've stopped sinning. It means you've declared war on your sin, stepped into the ring to fight with the power and grace of the Holy Spirit. Discipline is what is required to pick you back up when you lay down and stop fighting, and especially when you refuse to fight. When you call a truce with your sin, discipline is the reminder that surrender is not an option for those who are in Christ. This life is war!

---

2   See Ephesians 2:8-9

3   See Jude 1

4   Matthew 10:38-39, 16:24-26, Mark 8:34-38, Luke 14:25-33,

5   Attributed to Jonathan Leeman

The path of repentance

Let's start with a working definition of the final act of church discipline. *The culmination of church discipline is the act of removing an individual from membership in the church and participation in the Lord's Supper due to that individual's refusal to repent of serious sin.* It is the withdrawal of the church's affirmation of a person's claim to be a follower of Christ. Sometimes it's referred to as 'excommunication' because the church has 'ex-communed' them from the Lord's Table.

As important as it is to say what church discipline is, it's also important to say what it is not. When a church acts to discipline someone, they aren't saying definitively that person is *not* a Christian. They are saying they can no longer affirm that individual's personal profession of faith in the Lord Jesus. They aren't consigning them to eternal judgment in the Roman Catholic sense. As we discussed in chapter 1, the church's power is declaratory. The church speaks on Christ's behalf, but isn't Christ Himself. We cannot see into the heart of man and cannot make eternal judgment. We hope and pray the person will repent and turn to Christ.

Church discipline also isn't some form of shunning or shaming like the Amish or Mormons. It's not a barring of the doors to keep an individual from coming to church services. On the contrary, that's exactly where we want them to be, sitting under the preaching, teaching, singing, and praying of the Word of God, and seeing the Word of God in the ordinances. The 'church gathered' welcomes and invites all sinners to hear and see the gospel.

The church is a hospital for the sick in need of healing. But church membership is not a place for those who refuse to admit they are sick with sin. The church proclaims the gospel by displaying repentance and faith in Jesus Christ to the world. Repentance and faith are worked out and walked out in the everyday lives of her members. The church must keep the gospel pure. Church membership isn't for sinless perfect people. It's for repentant people. A lack of repentance muddies the waters and sullies the gospel.

When a member of a local church does not repent, the church has a responsibility to respond. That response should be in the everyday interactions between brothers and sisters ninety-nine percent of the time. This is why healthy relationships in the church are so necessary. We need people who love us enough to point out when we are on the wrong track. We need older women who can model for us and warn us of hazards in the Christian life. We need sisters to keep us accountable and shore us up when doubts come our way. Do you have those kinds of relationships? Are you building deep, transparent friendships in your local church? Without brotherly (and sisterly) love and affection, church discipline will become a rod of anger and abuse, not a tool of compassionate correction.

Getting personal

So what do we do when someone in the church seriously sins against us personally? What is the proper course of action? Should you go directly to them, confronting them on their wrongdoing? Should you share it (with all the sordid details) with a handful of your friends under the guise of seeking 'wisdom and prayer?' God's Word gives us a play by play for this very situation. Matthew 18:15-17 states:

> If your brother sins against you, go and tell him his fault, between you and him alone. If he listens to you, you have gained your brother. But if he does not listen, take one or two others along with you, that every charge may be established by the evidence of two or three witnesses. If he refuses to listen to them, tell it to the church. And if he refuses to listen even to the church, let him be to you as a Gentile and a tax collector.

Jesus' first concern is that the sinner repents. *Repentance is the goal*. It's no accident that this passage comes right after the parable of the lost sheep who is found. But Jesus is also concerned with *reconciliation* and *restoration*. He gives us steps to proceed with confronting someone in their sin, *keeping the circle as small as possible for as long as possible*. This reduces the possibility of gossip and slander and so protects unity in the body and the reputation of Christ. Given our own wrestling with sin, being honest without self-righteousness can be difficult. If our goal is God's glory in restoring someone to Christ, then we will fight hard to keep that circle of knowledge small and our knowledge of our own sin big. We might need counsel, but we also need to check our own hearts. Often our search for counsel turns into a gossip ring to share information more than a genuine desire to gain wisdom.

We should move forward *gently, patiently, tearfully, faithfully, quietly (at first) and then corporately*. Our words should always be 'seasoned with salt'[6] and measured with God's Word so we display a spirit of gentleness.[7] Private rebukes, even when delivered with love and affection, are still hard to hear. James tells us to be 'quick to hear, slow to speak, slow to anger.'[8] Questions ought to precede accusations. We often lack the full scope of another's situation, so questions make things clearer to us as we move forward. We should be broken about someone's hardening to their sin. There is no place for a proud, self-righteous disciple. We're all hell-deserving sinners. The fact that God hasn't already dealt with us as we deserve is an enormous mercy. Humility and dependence upon God should mark us as we confront someone in their sin. There is always hope that God will soften the heart.

If there is no repentance one on one or with two or three confronting the brother or sister, it is the work of the congregation to step in and speak on behalf of Jesus. Jesus says in Matthew 18 that the last step is to take it to the church. He doesn't say take

---

6   Colossians 1:6

7   Galatians 6:1

8   James 1:19

it to the elders. He says 'tell it to the church.' Likewise, Paul in 1 Corinthians 5 doesn't rebuke the elders for their inaction. He rebukes the church! He commands the church to take action when they're assembled. This is part of their job as members of a local church. God is not merely interested in people who make a 'decision for Christ' but in those who are becoming disciples of Christ. He's concerned about the holiness of the church.

Salt and light

Behind Jesus' teaching in Matthew 18 is the assumption that Christians are to be the salt of the earth and a light to the world.[9] As Christians we are to be *distinct*, set apart by the quality of our lives. When our lives no longer demonstrate a hatred for sin and a true repentant heart, we mar Christ's name to the world. This is what Jesus means when He compares the unrepentant sinner to an unclean Gentile and a traitorous tax collector. It's here where Matthew 18 plays itself out in real time. Paul picks up on this same teaching of church discipline in multiple places in his letters: Galatians 5:10, 6:1; 2 Thessalonians 3:6-15; 1 Timothy 5:19-22; and Titus 3:9-11. But the clearest is in 1 Corinthians 5:1-5, 12-13:

> It is actually reported that there is sexual immorality among you, and of a kind that is not tolerated even among pagans, for a man has his father's wife. And you are arrogant! Ought you not rather to mourn? Let him who has done this be removed from among you. For though absent in body, I am present in spirit; and as if present, I have already pronounced judgment on the one who did such a thing. When you are assembled in the name of the Lord Jesus and my spirit is present, with the power of our Lord Jesus, you are to deliver this man to Satan for the destruction of the flesh, so that his spirit may be saved in the day of the Lord....For what have I to do with judging outsiders? Is it not those inside the church whom you are to

---

9   Matthew 5:13-16, Mark 9:50, Luke 8:16,

judge? God judges those outside. 'Purge the evil person from among you.

The Corinthians valued power and position in their congregants more than the purity and holiness of Christ's church.[10] Thus, Paul says four different times that they are to judge the man by removing him or disciplining him from the church. But why? Did Paul hate the man? Is the church to no longer love him? Not at all! It was because he was so deeply deceived. He thought he could not only deliberately disobey the Lord, but flaunt that disobedience, and still call himself a Christian. So out of concern for his soul, and for the souls of those he could lead astray, they must act to withdraw the name of Christ from him. They are 'to deliver this man to Satan for the destruction of the flesh, so that his spirit may be saved in the day of the Lord' (v. 5). The goal is restoration. Restoration of the purity of the church and restoration of the man's soul.

Why go through the fuss?

Church discipline is hard, heavy, and often messy work. So why go through all the fuss? Why risk potentially alienating people or stirring up division? Why not just keep the peace? There are at least five reasons churches should be practicing church discipline.

First, we should do it for the benefit of the one being disciplined. The man in 1 Corinthians 5 thought he could call himself a Christian and yet live as he pleased. He needed to be warned lest he be deceived and perish eternally. The purpose of discipline is never retributive, but always restorative. It is never loving to leave someone in their sins. It's a means to expose their sins and warn them of a greater judgment to come.[11]

---

10 Numerous scholars think they endured, maybe even celebrated the sin *because* the man was of high-standing. They felt honored to have him, so they were willing to overlook his sins.

11 1 Corinthians 5:5

In 2 Corinthians 2 we see church discipline that has yielded fruit. Paul writes to the church, '[T]his punishment by the majority is enough…forgive and comfort him…I beg you to reaffirm your love for him' (vv. 6-8). Apparently, the man being disciplined repented of his sin, so Paul tells the church to forgive and restore him to fellowship. This man wandered from the truth but church discipline brought him back, to the benefit of his soul.

Second, we do it for the benefit of other members of the church. When we tolerate open, grievous sin in our midst, we are teaching one another that such behavior is acceptable for a Christian. This is why Paul warns the Galatian church when dealing with someone caught in a transgression, 'Keep watch on yourself, lest you too be tempted' (Gal. 6:1). Paul lays out how to protect the church in his first letter to Timothy. 'As for those[12] who persist in sin, rebuke them in the presence of all' (5:20). And notice the reason for this public rebuke, 'so that the rest may stand in fear.' The public rebuke of an unrepentant sinner shows all the members of the church that God cares about their purity. It upholds a right fear of God. Church discipline, rightly practiced, benefits every member of the church.

Third, we practice church discipline for the protection of the whole church. As Paul warned the Corinthians, 'Do you not know a little leaven leavens the whole lump? Cleanse out the old leaven that you may be a new lump' (1 Cor. 5.6-7). As a little bit of yeast spreads through and affects the whole lump of dough, unrepentant sin left unaddressed can spread and affect the whole church. Paul urges the church to celebrate, 'not with the old leaven, the leaven of malice and evil, but with the unleavened bread of sincerity and truth' (v. 8). Imagine malice and evil worming their way into the church, infecting the health and unity of the body of believers. Church discipline protects the health of the whole church.

Fourth, we do it for the corporate witness of the church. Churches are to be embassies of the kingdom of God, outposts in

---

12   1 Timothy 5:19-20 specifically addresses charges against an elder.

the world, displaying who God is and what He is like. When we tolerate unrepentant sin in our midst, we're confusing the world. The world can't see what God is like. They can't see what it means to be a Christian. This undermines our evangelistic witness by giving unbelievers a distorted view of the gospel. Mark Dever states it clearly, 'Jesus intended our lives to back up our words. If our lives don't back up our words, the evangelistic task is injured, as we have seen so terribly this last century in America. Undisciplined churches have actually made it harder for people to hear the Good News of new life in Jesus Christ.'[13] If the church is no different than the world, why bother with her?

Last, and most importantly, we practice church discipline for the glory of God. God cares deeply about the purity of His church. Christ died for it! Ephesians 5:22-33 is often read and preached at weddings, as it lays out the responsibilities of husbands and wives. But a deeper look at this passage shows us that it is more fundamentally about Christ and His church.[14] In fact, marriage itself is meant to image Christ and the church. In the passage, Paul explains why Christ died:

> Husbands, love your wives, as Christ loved the church and gave himself up for her, that he might sanctify her, having cleansed her by the washing of water with the word, so that he might present the church to himself in splendor, without spot or wrinkle or any such thing, that she might be holy and without blemish (vv. 25-27).

Christ gave Himself up for the church, to sanctify her. His aim is to present her as His spotless bride, holy and without blemish. The purity of the church shows the world we are His.

---

13 Dever, Mark; *Nine Marks of a Healthy Church*, (Wheaton, IL: Crossway, 2004), p. 179

14 Ephesians 5:32

Our churches act as billboard signs to the world advertising Christ. We reflect His character in how we live our lives together. Church discipline tells the world that we follow Christ and want His glory to be known. Peter pressed this point home when he wrote to the suffering and beleaguered persecuted saints. Even in their trial he understood how vital their holiness in the church was for their gospel witness. He writes in 1 Peter 2:12 (NIV), 'Live such good lives among the pagans that, though they accuse you of doing wrong, they may see your good deeds and glorify God on the day he visits us.' Our fight for holiness is how we defend and protect God's reputation. It's the wedding ring that we show to prove we are His. Church discipline is for the glory of God.

A blunt instrument

Over the years, I've become quite handy around the house. When our dishwasher broke this month, my sweet husband looked at it for a minute, sighed, and suggested I call out for a repair. (He'll be the first to tell you he feels much more comfortable with a book than a power tool!) But I managed to identify the problem, order the part, take the washer apart, and fix it. (Thanks to some help from YouTube.) One thing I've learned along the way is the importance of the right tool. You don't want to use a drill if a Phillips screwdriver will fit the bill. You don't need a jack-hammer when a simple rubber mallet will do. So it is in the church. The final act of church discipline is a broad, blunt instrument. Like that jack-hammer, you only wield it when absolutely necessary. *We shouldn't be afraid to use it, but we shouldn't be too eager either.*

Under what conditions, then, should we remove a member from the church roll? This final act of church discipline should only be used when the sin is *serious*, *demonstrable*, and *unrepentant*.

The sin must be serious enough to warrant a serious response. Fear and anxiety might be sins, but we shouldn't publicly discipline for them. There needs to be plenty of room for Peter's reminder that 'love covers a multitude of sins' (1 Pet. 4:8). God calls us to forbear with one another. We are all sinners and we all stumble each and every day. One of the hallmark signs of a healthy church is forgiving and bearing with one another in great love. Discipline should be reserved for significant sins that bring disrepute on the gospel, publicly dishonor Christ, or significantly undermine one's Christian testimony. What is hard about this category is its subjectivity. How do we determine if a sin is causing disrepute upon the gospel? Doesn't all sin in effect dishonor Christ? Congregations, and especially the elders who lead them, need His wisdom to discern situations and rightly assess them with godliness and charity. The wonderful promise we have from God is that He has given us the mind of Christ (1 Cor. 2:16).

The sin also must be demonstrable. It must have an outward, visible nature to it. It must be obvious enough to be able to see it with our eyes or hear it with our ears. The facts should be indisputable. This isn't a place for 'he said', 'she said' kind of situations. This means we likely aren't disciplining for things like pride and greed. Are those sins serious? Yes! But are they demonstrable? That's harder to determine. Take greed. Maybe they stole significantly from their employer, in which case it is demonstrable. But a large house and nice things? That could be a sign of greed, but they also may use them very well for ministry. Being wealthy isn't a sin. Dragging the church into such conversations will rarely be fruitful or helpful. When it comes to the blunt instrument of church discipline, it ought to be more objective and clear, more black and white than shades of gray. Was there an affair? Are they refusing to come to church? Are they repeatedly drunk? Did they embezzle from their employer? Such sins are more demonstrable.

Most importantly, the sinner must be unrepentant! Churches should never discipline a repentant person. Every member of a church is a sinner and should be a repenting sinner. We want church members to be open about their sin and seek help from their brothers and sisters, not hide their sin and let it fester. *Church discipline is reserved for those who, in obstinance, refuse to turn from their sin.* They lie in the bed of sin they have made without any regard for getting out of it. This is what we see in the two examples we have in Scripture in Matthew 18 and 1 Corinthians 5. Both of these people held themselves out to be Christians, yet still persisted in serious, clear, and unrepentant sin.

Jesus makes it clear that true repentance is drastic, it cuts off a hand, gouges out an eye. It does whatever is necessary to put sin to death (cf. Matt. 5:.29-30). Truly repentant people are willing to inconvenience themselves for Jesus.

In Paul's second letter to the Corinthian church he mentions the grief he caused them by his first letter, but that grief (or sorrow) bore good fruit through their repentance and change of action. He wrote to them:

> For even if I made you grieve with my letter, I do not regret it – though I did regret it, for I see that that letter grieved you, though only for a while. I rejoice, not because you were grieved, but because you were grieved into repenting. For you felt godly grief, so that you suffered no loss through us. For godly grief produces a repentance that leads to salvation without regret, whereas worldly grief produces death. (2 Cor. 7:8-9)

The godly grief of repentance led them to change. Worldly sorrow pays lip service to grief. It grieves only the consequences of sin, bears no lasting results, and evidences no fruit of true repentance and change.

The question we have to keep in front of us when we are walking with our fellow member in sin is, 'Is he or she truly repenting, or just paying lip service?' This kind of discernment, distinguishing between godly and worldly sorrow, takes great wisdom from God. We need His Word to inform and direct our hearts to discern the motives. (This is why God gave elders to His church. These godly men can help lead us when we are faced with unusual circumstances and situations, when the pathway to proceed isn't as clear as we would like it to be.) The church should only discipline for unrepentant sin.

Finally, we only discipline those who are members of our churches. In verses 12-13 of 1 Corinthians 5, Paul is very clear that we are only to judge those inside the church and not outside. This means we certainly don't discipline non-Christians, for they don't hold themselves out to be Christians. And we don't discipline visitors and guests. They may loosely profess Christ, but how do we know if we haven't intentionally heard their testimony, confirmed their understanding of the gospel, and formally welcomed them into fellowship? We are called to make judgments on members who have professed faith in the Lord Jesus and have committed to us, and we have committed to them. We don't make judgments on non-members or non-Christians.

The final act of church discipline is not to be taken lightly but in some cases it must be taken to protect the church. Removing a member from the body of believers is painful. Yet, one who refuses to repent of serious, demonstrable sin has no legitimate place in the church. Louis Berkof notes:

> There is a very evident tendency to stress the fact that the Church is a great missionary agency, and to forget that it is first of all the assembly of the saints, in which those who publicly live in sin cannot be tolerated. It is said that sinners must be gathered into the church, and not excluded from it. But it should be remembered that they must be gathered in as saints and have no legitimate place in the Church as long as they do not *confess* their sin and strive for holiness.[15] (emphasis mine)

---

15 Berkof, Louis; *Systematic Theology*, (Edinburgh: Banner of Truth Trust, 2000) p. 601

The church is an assembly of saints, sinners saved by grace. We exist as the body of Christ to display the glory of God. Church discipline keeps that glory shining.

Let all be done in love

Now that we have a clearer picture of the ins and outs of church discipline – what it is and isn't, why we should do it, when we should do it and how we should do it, the final question worth considering is: how are we to treat someone who's been disciplined by the church? Looking back at the text we considered earlier in 1 Corinthians 5, Paul says we are not to associate with them, not even to eat with them (v. 11-12). In 2 Thessalonians 3, he says, 'keep away from any brother who is walking in idleness and not in accord with the tradition that you received from us' (v. 6) and 'have nothing to do with him, that he may be ashamed' (v. 14). Likewise, Jesus says we're to regard them as, 'a Gentile and a tax collector' (Matt. 18.17).

But looking closer at the texts, Paul and Jesus are not encouraging withdrawing our love from the person who is disciplined or some kind of shaming or shunning. These texts are about no longer affirming their profession for Christ. They are saying we're not to continue our regular relationships with them as if nothing has happened. This is not a time for casual conversations and hanging out because the brother or sister continues to claim the name of Christ and yet live in open sin. There should be discomfort and a sense of awkwardness in conversing with them casually. Conversations should be intentionally focused around their spiritual health and profession of faith, calling them back to Christ. If discipline involves a person in someone's own biological family, they can, and should, continue to fulfill family obligations.[16] Breaking the church covenant relationship doesn't equal the breaking of a family relationship. Most importantly, we should be praying regularly and

---

16   Ephesians 6:1-3. 1 Timothy 5:8, 1 Peter 3:1-2

hopefully for God to bring about repentance and restoration of our disciplined brother or sister.

Now if that brother or sister does repent, then rejoice! His or her soul has been saved from death.[17] They are to be welcomed back joyfully! Of course, caution must be used. Knowing whether or not true repentance has occurred often requires time. But once *true* repentance is established, they are to be brought back into the fold where forgiveness is pronounced, as well as affirmation of love for them.[18] We shouldn't enforce a long probationary or parole period or brand them with a scarlet letter. We should instead celebrate over them as the Father did over the prodigal son.[19] When the world sees this kind of restoration happen, the truth of the gospel story is overwhelmingly clear! As the church faithfully carries out their duties in this way, the gospel witness to the world is upheld and this kind of restoration should mimic the rejoicing of the shepherd who found the one lost sheep and returned him to the ninety-nine at home.

In the end, discipline is about love. For God disciplines those He loves (Heb. 12:6). He does it for our good, that we may share in His holiness (Heb. 12:11). The reality that we are all in the muck and mire of our sin should give us compassion for one another and unite us to help each other on our journey to heaven. There is zero space for pride or arrogance. We are all debtors of God's great mercy. Discipline is painful, but pays dividends in the end, not only for the individual disciplined or the members of the church, but also for her public witness. It's about making sure that Jesus's representatives on earth are actually representing Him and not someone or something else.[20] For the church that fails to practice church discipline will

---

17 James 5:20

18 2 Corinthians 2:6-8

19 Luke 15:24

20 Leeman, Jonathan, *Church Discipline: How the Church Protects the Name of Jesus* (Wheaton, IL: Crossway, 2012), p. 23

one day become a church that looks eerily similar to the world, so like the unbelievers in the world, they won't have anything to ask us. It's why pastor and theologian, J.L. Dagg, once ominously said, 'When discipline leaves a church, Christ goes with it.' Church discipline is necessary for the purity of God's church.

We fight for this purity through the practice of church discipline, but we also fight for it in the ways we conduct ourselves individually in the world and collectively as a people of God; the unity we display together. Our public witness matters both privately and corporately. Just as the purity of the church is imperative, so is her unity.

Unity: An array of color

I'm not a gardener, but I have big goals to become one someday! One of my favorite things is when a garden is overflowing in its diversity of flora. Layers of colors, shapes, sizes and varieties all together in a marvelous display of 'controlled chaos,' as my husband likes to call it. Much like a garden, God created the church to be a beautiful and attractive picture of His glory to the world. There is a unity in the diversity she displays in God's good design of His church. And this beautiful design is highlighted when God's people live lives of holiness together in all their diversity. *The visible church represents invisible realities to the world.* Our unity in diversity as a church is inextricably tied to the purity of the lives of her members and their collective affirmation of gospel truths.[21] Ephesians 3:10 says, 'that through the church the manifold wisdom of God might now be made known to the rulers and authorities in the heavenly places.' God's manifold wisdom is seen in the diversity from which He saved us and the way He saved us.

---

21 Derivatives from thoughts on holiness taken from Jonathan Leeman's chapter, 'A Congregational Approach to Unity, Holiness, and Apostolicity.' *Baptist Foundations*, p. 337, 343

As we've just discussed, the purity of a church's members is why church discipline is so important. So how does our unity fit in here? Where should our unity as a local church be found? Is it our preference of music? Our decision to homeschool or send our children to public school? Whether or not we work outside the home? What about ethnicity? Should these be the essential issues that unify us?

During the early years of the church some began teaching you had to become a Jew first in order to become a Christian. 'Unless you are circumcised according to the custom of Moses, you *cannot be saved*' (Acts 15:1, emphasis mine). 'It is *necessary* to circumcise them and to *order them* to keep the law of Moses' (Acts 15:5 emphasis mine). Such commands caused great debate and division within the fledgling church. They threatened to segregate congregations into Jewish gatherings and separate Gentile gatherings. But notice the pressing issue wasn't preferential or stylistic, but theological. For these false teachers wanted to make salvation a matter of human performance and religious obedience.

Some might say, 'Let them separate into separate congregations. Stop with the theological 'nitpicking' and let's get back on mission.' But not the apostles. For Peter stands and declares, 'God, who knows the heart, bore witness to them [Gentiles], by giving them the Holy Spirit just as he did to us, and he made *no distinction* between us and them, having cleansed their hearts by faith' (Acts 15:8-9, emphasis mine). Peter's final words in the book of Acts are to clarify the gospel, and the shared unity we have in that gospel. He's helping us see that Christian unity is first and foremost *gospel* unity.

This is why Paul urged the Ephesian church to '...walk in a manner worthy of the calling to which you have been called, with all humility and gentleness, with patience, bearing with one another in love, eager to maintain the **unity** (emphasis mine) of the Spirit in the bond of peace. There is one body and one Spirit - just as you were called to the one hope that belongs to your call- one Lord, one faith, one baptism, one God and Father of all, who is over all and through all and in all' (Eph. 4:1-6). Our unity displays the unity of God Himself. The collective, corporate affirmation of Gospel truths is at the heart of this unity.

It's why Paul also opposed Peter to his face when he separated himself from the Gentile Christians and began eating only with Jewish Christians (Gal. 2.11-14). The New Testament writers give many strong warnings against those who cause divisions. Paul, in Romans 16:17-18, writes, 'I appeal to you, brothers, to watch out for those who cause divisions and create obstacles contrary to the doctrine that you have been taught; avoid them. For such persons do not serve our Lord Christ, but their own appetites, and by smooth talk and flattery they deceive the hearts of the naive.' As believers we are to live in unity because of our spiritual unity in Christ Himself.

Without an anchor stuck deep into the truth of the gospel the wind and waves of the world's 'philosophies and empty deceit' will unmoor us (Col. 2:8). We'll be tempted to shift our focus from essential things to non-essential things, resulting in infighting, disunity, and ultimately a failed gospel witness. Theologian Gerald Bray states, 'For Protestants, learning to distinguish between what is essential and what is not is vitally important if the unity of the church is to be preserved and the truth of the gospel maintained. If nonessentials are allowed to become matters of debate that divide the church, the likelihood is that people will focus on them rather than on the far more important matters directly connected to the gospel.'[22]

The unity we strive for in the church must be tightly wrapped around the truth of the gospel. This means the bond we experience as members of a church should not be marked by ethnicity, age,

---

22   Bray, Gerald, *God is Lord: A Biblical & Systematic Theology* (Wheaton, IL: Crossway, 2012), p. 663

or sex. It shouldn't be marked by race, socioeconomic status, education, or any other distinguishing characteristic created by mankind, including musical preferences! God delights to demonstrate His love through a diverse group of people He has called to be one in Himself. 'In Christ there is not Greek and Jew, circumcision and uncircumcision, barbarian, Scythian, slave and free; but Christ is all and in all.'[23]

Many churches today pride themselves on their distinctive style. Some even divide their gatherings into categories. Attenders can choose between a traditional or contemporary service; and, no thanks to the prolonged Covid season, many can now choose between in person or virtual. Where we live here in Arkansas there are churches for cowboys and churches for motorcyclists! In a celebrity culture that prided itself on charismatic personalities and were dividing over those personalities (1 Cor. 1.11-12), Paul questioned, 'Is Christ divided? Was Paul crucified for you? Or were you baptized into the name of Paul?' Notice Paul's reasoning isn't merely practical, but theological. Paul is saying: Is the church a divided house with different saviors? Did anybody other than Christ save you? Was anyone other than Christ crucified for you? All rhetorical questions for which the obvious answer is 'No!' Therefore, why are you dividing over human personalities? Such was Paul's concern for the gospel unity of the church. His concern wasn't just to make Christians happy, but that Christ would be honored among the nations.

In 1 Corinthians 12 Paul helpfully illustrates this grand design of beauty and harmony in diversity when he describes the variety of gifts within the church. 'For just as the body is one and has many members, and all the members of the body, through many, are one body, so it is with Christ. For in one Spirit we were all baptized into one body – Jews and Greeks, slave or free – and all were made to

---

23   Colossians 3:11, CSB. See also Romans 10:12

drink of one Spirit.'[24] Because in the church the many are made one in Christ by the Spirit, there should be unity. Whether divisible by ethnic categories (Jew or Greek) or worldly categories (slave or free), they are one in the body. Each part of the body has a role and each role needs the other in order to function best.[25]

This is not to say that Christians will never divide. There are doctrines that are not essential for salvation, but are essential for gathering together. Doctrines such as baptism (Do we baptize only believers, or believers and their children?),[26] or church government (Who governs? A bishop, the elders, the congregation?).[27] Obedience to Christ means in such cases we will gather in separate congregations this side of heaven. But we must not let those distinctions overshadow the unity we have in the gospel. In the words of a beloved pastor, 'Fidelity to Christ means we must erect doctrinal walls, but we must be willing to reach over those walls and shake-hands as much as possible.' Or as the often misapplied, but still helpful quote goes, 'In essentials unity, in non-essentials liberty, and in all things charity.'[28]

The curious visitor

Imagine with me a church service where a visitor sneaks in the back. Curious about who really goes to church anymore, she looks around and sees men and women of all ages. They make up different nationalities and there are families, singles, college students, single parents, people with special needs, some who seem to be wealthy, others are pierced and tattooed, but there is palpable joy and love for one another that transcends any of those differences. The visitor

24   1 Corinthians 12:12-13

25   Refer to chapter 3 for a fuller discussion on the body of Christ

26   Refer to chapter 5 for a fuller discussion on baptism

27   Refer to chapter 7 for a fuller discussion on church government

28   Attributed to German Lutheran theologian of the early seventeenth century, Rupertus Meldenius

might think to herself, 'What in the world is going on here? This is a strange community of people.' And as she continues to observe she notes how they seem to genuinely care for one another, reaching across social, racial, financial and physical divides. It's here that a profound declaration of God's unifying work in the hearts of His people is on full display, testifying to His love and care for His people.[29]

When the people of God live lives of holiness and love for one another in the community of a local church, it is one of the most powerful apologetics for the gospel. All the parts of the body work together as the Lord designed. It demonstrates visibly what we share verbally about the gospel. It's powerful! The world can't explain how a diverse group of people can have such unity. That unity and the purity of the church is so attractive it cannot be ignored.

29 Dever, Mark and Dunlop, Jamie. *The Compelling Community: Where God's Power Makes a Church Attractive* (Wheaton, IL: Crossway, 2015).

Questions

'A Pursuit of Holiness: Church Unity and Discipline'

The world doesn't know what to make of a group of people unified yet diverse living lives of holiness together. When the purity of that group is protected by the practice of church discipline and care is given to maintain the unity of the corporate body, they impact the world around them with the gospel.

1. What are the two forms of discipline? Which one is most often seen practiced in the Bible and the church?

2. How would you explain the final act of church discipline to a friend?

3. How should you handle a situation where a brother or sister in the church sins against you? What passage of Scripture could you use to help instruct and guide you in that process?

4. Why should churches practice church discipline, and what should be the motivation behind it?

5. We shouldn't be too afraid to use discipline, but we shouldn't be too eager, either. What are four conditions that we can use to guide when it should be used?

6. What must be the primary motivation behind practicing church discipline?

7. What does it mean to be unified?

8. What should the church be unified around?

9. How does unity in our diversity demonstrate the gospel to others?

10. Is it okay to divide over some things? If so, what things are worth dividing over?

Chapter 7

A Flock With a Job to Do:
Congregationalism, Elders, and Deacons

We long to see thy churches full,
That all the chosen race,
May, with one voice and heart and soul,
Sing Thy redeeming grace.

'How Sweet & Aweful'
Isaac Watts

Authority. It's not a four letter word, but for many it might as well be. If we're honest with ourselves we often feel suspect when we're confronted with authority, don't we? It doesn't take much looking around or living too long to see authority figures and structures that have grossly mishandled their role. Many have provoked fear or suspicion. Others have gone so far as to harm or abuse those under their leadership. A boss who cheats, a pastor who manipulates, a president who lies, a husband who abandons, a church who neglects, a parent who hits, a teacher who favors, a priest who molests, and the list could go on and on. We're horrified when we read about the abuse of authority in the world and long not only for justice, but for righteous authority to prevail. Authority rightly exercised can be a palace of protection. Wrongly exercised it can be a world of frustration or worse, torture. Power exercised outside of God's plans and purposes is demonic.

I remember the first time I read the familiar words of Lord Acton in his letter to Bishop Creighton in 1887: 'Power tends to corrupt and absolute power corrupts absolutely.' It was my eighth-grade civics class and we were talking about abuses by political authorities. It would take a few decades for me to grasp the weight of his words, but one thing was clear. They seemed to carry more truth than I wanted them to.

But should we eschew all authority? Should we be thinking about authority in this way in regards to the church? Is church-exercised authority inherently harmful and dangerous? If not, what should authority structures (or polity) in the church look like, and how should it function? These are some of the topics this chapter will address.

Some of you reading might already feel an overwhelming urge to skip this chapter. A class on church 'civics'? No thank you! But might I encourage you to read on just a little further? I hope to convince you that while church polity isn't the gospel, it is meant to protect and preserve that gospel, and thus is far more important than you may realize. Like that precious diamond carefully set into the prongs of a ring, so the gospel diamond is held up and secured for all to see by the structure of church governance.

At the outset, there are many brothers and sisters in the faith whom I deeply respect and admire who hold different views from me. That said, I strongly believe the Bible clearly teaches that the authority of the church is given to the congregation and her elders.

I'd even go so far as to say elder-led congregationalism is God's design. It's His discipling program for the church.

Congregationalism

In chapter 3 we considered God's plan for redemptive history and how, as image bearers, He created man and woman and placed them in a garden to work and watch over it (Gen. 2:15). Right there in the Garden of Eden He gave men and women a job. They were to keep the garden, where God dwelled with His people, safe from evil and harm, and then to fill the earth and subdue it. But they failed, and miserably so. In their rebellion they were thrust from the garden and were consigned to physical and spiritual death. But God wasn't finished with His people or His plans. Just as God had called Adam to Himself, so He would call a people to Himself and dwell with them in the temple. And He would call these people to work and watch over this dwelling place, such that they would be a kingdom of priests, a holy nation, set apart and consecrated to God.[1] But sadly, they too would fail. So God would send His own Son, Jesus Christ, in order to dwell again with His people. Unlike the first Adam, Jesus perfectly fulfilled the commands of His Father. By dying on the cross as a substitute for sinners He made the way to permanently dwell with His chosen people.

The church is the temple of the New Testament where God's people gather in His name, and under His authority. In 1 Corinthians 3:16, Paul writes, 'Do you not know that you (Corinthian church) are God's temple and that God's Spirit dwells in you? If anyone destroys God's temple, God will destroy him. For God's temple is holy, and you are that temple.'[2] The local church is what we, as God's chosen people, indwelt by the Holy Spirit, are called to work and watch over. Like Adam and Eve we are to be fruitful and multiply, but as a church we do so by going and making disciples, baptizing

1   Numbers 3:7-8

2   See also 1 Cor 5.4; Eph 2.2

them and teaching them to obey all that Jesus commanded. That is our job description. Before Jesus gave the church these marching orders, He said, 'All authority in heaven and on earth has been given to me' (Matt. 28:18). The job description of the church is rooted in Jesus' authority.

THE BUCK STOPS HERE

We've already seen that in Matthew 16, upon Peter's confession of Jesus as the Christ, Jesus gives Peter, and subsequently the church, their job. With their job description comes the authority to carry out the duties entrusted to their care. They are to watch over the Kingdom of God and work for its expansion here on earth. In Matthew 18:18 we've seen these keys of the kingdom – given to bind and loose – were intended not just for Peter and the apostles, but they were given to the local church.[3] That means that every single member of the church is tasked with the high calling of declaring what the true gospel message is, according to God's Word, and who God's people truly are. Matthew 18:17-20 shows us that Jesus gave this authority to the local church, not just to individual Christians.

Congregationalism is the understanding that in local church life, the final court of appeal is not the bishop of Rome, a college of cardinals, or one's denominational headquarters. It's not a convention or regional synod. It isn't even the pastor or the elders. The last and final court of appeal is the congregation. The buck stops with them. Jesus said 'tell it to the church' (Matt. 18:17). Paul writes about 'the majority' making decisions (2 Cor. 2:6). In Acts 6, the apostles 'summoned the full number of disciples' (v. 2) to set apart men to take care of widows in the church. The church is responsible for the church. If then the congregation is the final authority, it is imperative we understand how that authority is to be exercised.

---

3   Refer back to chapter 1 for further development of this idea.

Doctrine, Leadership, Membership, and Discipline

Do you remember the first time you were ever put in charge of anybody or anything? Maybe it was to look after your little brother in his highchair when your mom had to step out of the room to change the laundry. Or perhaps it was taking care of a puppy. My first babysitting job was frightening. I knew I was there to protect and watch out for these two little girls. The parents were in effect delegating their authority to me for a time, but I needed to know their expectations so I could carry out my job appropriately. Having the directions in front of me from their parents gave me relief and a sense of clarity on exactly what I was to do while they were away. Our Heavenly Father has, in His Word, given us our job responsibilities. There are four areas that I believe Scripture lays out for churches to exercise delegated authority from Jesus: doctrine, leadership, membership and discipline. Let's look at each one of these areas.

First, congregations exercise their authority in the area of _doctrine_. The church is called the 'pillar and buttress of the truth' (1 Tim. 3:15). She is built on the foundation of the Scriptures (Eph. 2:20) and is responsible for protecting the gospel. This is why, in Galatians 1, we read Paul's frustration with false teaching infiltrating the church. He says, 'I am astonished that you are so quickly deserting him who called you in the grace of Christ and are turning to a different gospel.'[4] What's of note for us here is to whom Paul is appealing. He's appealing 'to the churches of Galatia' (1:1), not just the elders of the churches in Galatia! The 'you' in verse 6 is plural, like a southern 'y'all'. Likewise, in 2 Timothy 4:2-4 he tells Timothy to preach the Word and places the responsibility on the congregation to listen. He says, 'For the time is coming when people will not endure sound teaching, but having itching ears they will accumulate for themselves teachers to suit their own passions, and will turn away from listening to the truth and wander off into

---

4   Galatians 1:6

THE DOCTRINE OF THE CHURCH, FOR EVERY WOMAN

myths' (vv. 3-4). This letter to Timothy would have been read to the church and then circulated among the churches. Paul is telling the church that their participation in sitting under this false teaching and supporting it financially makes them as guilty as the one who is teaching it. The focus of all the pastoral epistles is teaching sound doctrine so that the church can recognize false. This is how a local church can be 'a pillar and buttress of the truth.'

No matter the history or connections we may have with a church, we must never support a ministry that is subverting or distorting the gospel message. Don't support it with your time, your money, or your presence! This is why you must care about your church's statement of faith. We tend to think statements of faith are only for theologians and pastors. But as we've seen it's not just pastors who are responsible for the church's doctrine. According to Paul, you, as a church member, will be held accountable for the doctrine your church holds and teaches. Congregationalism puts guardrails around the gospel.

This leads us to the second area in which the church exercises authority. We exercise our congregational authority in the area of _church leadership_. This authority flows from the church's authority to keep their doctrine pure. It is the congregation's privilege and responsibility to be sure the elders (pastors) who are appointed are equipped to lead and shepherd the congregation. In Acts 14:23 where Paul and Barnabas traveled to Lystra, Iconium and to Antioch, it says, 'And when they had appointed elders for them in every church, with prayer and fasting they committed them to the Lord in whom they had believed.' The word 'appoint' used here literally means 'by the raising of hands.' The sense we get is that such decisions were made with the consent of the congregation.

Elders, as we'll see later, are the teachers of the church. They are to teach sound doctrine.[5] The teaching of Scripture, and not what itching ears prefer to hear, guards the gospel and 'equip[s]

---

5   Titus 1:9

the saints for the work of ministry' (Eph. 4:12). Gospel teaching ensures the saints will 'no longer be children, tossed to and fro by the waves and carried about by every wind of doctrine, by human cunning, by craftiness in deceitful schemes' (v. 14). This is why the Bible gives specific qualifications and disqualifications for elders (see below). Churches appoint qualified elders who help to guard the true gospel of Christ. Members of churches are to see that qualified shepherds are established to teach and train the sheep.

The third area in which the church exercises authority is in matters of _membership_. We've actually already seen this in chapter 3. If the keys of the kingdom are in part to declare the 'who' of the gospel (namely who are gospel professors), and if Jesus conferred that authority to *congregations*, then *congregations* are responsible for declaring who is and isn't a member. This, not surprisingly, is exactly what we've see in 1 Corinthians 5. The congregation was to put the man outside the body. They withdraw him from membership in their family because he had forfeited his claim to Christ in the way he was living. In Paul's second letter to the Corinthians, we read in 2:6 that, 'this punishment by the *majority* is enough.' A 'majority' requires some kind of voting body and coming to a formal decision, an idea not uncommon to Greek city states. Paul encourages the church to forgive this repentant man and bring him back into membership. These passages aren't written to elders. They are written to the church. The church holds the keys to membership.

Seeing members in and out of the congregation is one of the job responsibilities of each member of the local church. This is why the members' meetings in my local church always begin with adding new members and removing members who are leaving the church. For our membership defines who we are as a body. To whom are we accountable? For whom are we responsible? Not the Christians who gather down the street, but our fellow members of our church. Membership matters are therefore the most important thing we handle each meeting. They're also one of my favorite parts of our life together as the elders present the testimonies of God's grace in the lives of these brothers and sisters. Following the time of acceptance of new members we turn to a time for removal from membership. This could be related to moving, death, or in the hard circumstances, church discipline. As members working together to protect the gospel witness to the world we 'own' our membership and see the vital importance of working together as a family.[6]

The last area we are called by God to exercise congregational authority in is the practice of _church discipline_. This goes along with our authority over membership. In our last chapter we discussed the role of church discipline in the life of a local church. For our purposes here, I want us to think of the final act of discipline by the whole church. This is not the day-to-day discipline that should be occurring in the lives of our brothers and sisters; the gentle rebuke or private confrontation about a matter of sin in one another's lives. I'm referring to that final step from chapter 6 of bringing serious, demonstrable, and unrepentant sin before the entire body of believers as described in Matthew 18:17. Again we see that Paul discusses the need for this kind of authority to be exercised in 1 Corinthians 5. He doesn't appeal to the elders or leaders, but calls the whole church assembled to respond to this man's flagrant and celebrated incestuous relationship: 'When you are assembled in the name of the Lord Jesus and my spirit is present, with the power of our Lord Jesus, you are to deliver this man to Satan, for the destruction of the flesh, so that his spirit may be saved on the day of the Lord' (1 Cor. 5.4-5). Who is the 'you' that is assembling and is to deliver the man over to Satan for the destruction of the flesh? It's the gathered _congregation_. It's the local church who is to remove that title of 'brother,' no longer affirming his profession of faith and removing him from the Lord's Supper. Further along in verses 12-13 Paul emphatically states, 'Is it not those inside the church whom

---

6   For a more thorough discussion on church membership, see chapter 2, 'A Gathering That Glorifies God'

you are to judge? God judges those outside. "Purge the evil person from among you."' The command to 'purge' is given not to deacons or the elders, or even the lead pastor, but the local congregation gathered. Discipline in the church is not just a pastoral matter, but finally a congregational matter.

God calls us to exercise our congregational authority over doctrine, leadership, membership and discipline. As members of local churches we're to work together to guard the gospel and see members and leaders in and out of the church. That is our primary job. The rug color won't have the same impact on our gospel witness as the actual members who represent the church. The seat cushion design won't protect gospel purity like the decision to hire a pastor who holds to the inerrancy and sufficiency of God's Word. A good rule of thumb would be to consider this principle: the closer a matter is to the spiritual health and vitality of the church, the more important it is for the congregation to exercise her authority in that regard. Her authority is from Jesus Himself so she must wield it well for Him.

SOME CAUTION

So now that we've established what congregationalism is and what congregations have authority over, let's turn and consider what congregationalism is not. First, congregationalism doesn't mean congregations are always right! All the New Testament letters to the churches and the pastoral epistles deal with some kind of error, either correcting, rebuking or warning against it. Congregationalism is biblical, for sure, but unlike the Bible, congregations aren't inerrant. The congregation that fired Jonathan Edwards, the preacher of the Great Awakening, for barring the unregenerate from the Lord's table, had the authority to do so, but that doesn't mean they were right when they did it. Congregationalism can be messy but it is God-ordained and keeps the church healthy when practiced rightly.

Second, congregationalism isn't a democracy. It has been argued that congregationalism is a mere byproduct of the Enlightenment.

But if we look back to Clement of Rome, Cyprian, and other early church fathers and writings, such as the Didache, they all supported congregationalism. Luther did so in the 1520s as did Congregationalists in Europe in the 15-1600s. This was before the rise of contemporary western-styled democracies. God's design for the church isn't like any one particular political structure. In fact, it functions more like a combination of monarchy (Jesus is king); oligarchy (a plurality of elders lead); and democracy (the congregation has final authority). It contains bits of all three of these governments with the Scriptures as the ruling documents.

Lastly, congregationalism isn't mob rule. This isn't a setting where every single matter in the church is up for a town hall debate. At its worst it can be. I've sat through members' meetings where every single jot and tittle were debated ad infinitum. Congregations are given pastors, by God, to lead, teach, and exercise authority while setting an example for the flock. In turn God calls those congregations to submit to their leaders (Heb. 13:17). The leadership of the church works in connection with the congregation. If we reject the good leadership God has put in place for us, we impede the work we can do as a church in the world today. This dance of submission to authority while practicing authority is unique. What does that look like? Let's turn now and consider the role of the elders and how they function in congruity with the congregation.

ELDERS

Depending on your background when you read the word 'elder' you might be thinking of an 'older' person or perhaps something more like a CEO. When you think about a board of elders you might be prone to imagine a board of trustees. When we look at the New Testament, however, we see a different picture take shape.

First, we see that elders occur in the plural. Paul and Barnabas see to it that the churches in Lystra, Iconium, and Antioch have 'elders' selected (see Acts 14:21-23). Luke speaks of the 'elders' in Ephesus in Acts 20:17. In Titus 1:5, Paul leaves Titus there in Crete to see that elders were established there in local churches. Whenever you see elders in the New Testament, you regularly see them in the plural. There isn't a prescribed number, but there should be more than one.

Secondly, the word elder can be used interchangeably with shepherd, pastor, and overseer.[7] In Acts 20, Paul addresses the 'elders' in v. 17, later referring to them as 'overseers' (where we get our English word 'bishop') in v. 28, and as those called to 'shepherd' (where we get our English word 'pastor'). Those words shepherd, pastor, overseer, and elder all refer to the same office.

Thirdly, we see that elders are gifts from God to His church (Eph. 4.11), not only to set an example (1 Pet. 5.3), but also to instruct, equip, and care for the local church. The congregation recognizes elders but the Holy Spirit makes them, as Paul stated in Acts 20:28. They are gifts God gives to His church.

ELDER QUALIFICATIONS

Paul gives specific requirements for elders. 1 Timothy 3:1-7 and Titus 1:5-9 offer a full list of qualifications. 1 Timothy says:

> [A]n overseer must be above reproach, the husband of one wife, sober-minded, self-controlled, respectable, hospitable, able to teach, not a drunkard, not violent but gentle, not quarrelsome, not a lover of money. He must manage his own household well, with all dignity keeping his children submissive...He must not be a recent convert...he must be well thought of by outsiders (1:2-7).

Titus adds characteristics like, not arrogant, but 'a lover of good,' 'upright, holy and disciplined' (vv. 7, 8).

---

7   See also 1 Peter 5:1-2, 4:11, 1 Timothy 3:1, Titus 1:7,

Elders are called to a long list of things that should honestly mark all believers. It's been noted that what's so exceptional about the qualifications, is just how unexceptional they are! The list of qualifications contains those things that would commend the gospel to a watching world. Paul repeats that an elder should be 'above reproach' (1 Tim. 3:2, Titus 1:6, 7) and says, 'he must be well thought of by outsiders' (1 Tim. 3:7). Elders should be models for the church and their lives should model the gospel for the world. This is why an elder 'must not be a recent convert' (v. 6). A recent convert hasn't had the time to grow as a Christian, and the church hasn't had enough time to observe his life and doctrine. There should be an established pattern of behavior that looks and smells like Jesus. Think of the apostles in Acts 4:13 when the people recognized that Peter and John 'had been with Jesus' in how they presented themselves. It takes time living in this world and with God's people for others to recognize that a man demonstrates the qualifications of an elder. His life must commend the gospel to the outside world and be a model for other believers to follow. His character matters![8]

The one qualification that goes beyond the characteristics that all believers should strive for is the _ability to teach_. 1 Timothy says, 'able to teach' and Titus says, 'He must hold firm to the trustworthy word as taught, so that he may be able to give instruction in sound doctrine and also to rebuke those who contradict it' (v. 9). Teaching is both a qualification and the role of an elder. This is why each of the pastoral epistles are filled with admonitions to teach. 'Teach and urge these things' (1 Tim. 6:2). '[P]reach the word...reprove, rebuke and exhort, with complete patience and teaching' (2 Tim. 4:2). '[T]each what accords with sound doctrine' (Titus 2:1). Through teaching and preaching, elders are to 'guard the good deposit,' the gospel of Jesus Christ that has been entrusted to the

---

8   See Aaron Menikoff, _Character Matters: Shepherding in the Fruit of the Spirit_ (Moody Publishers, Chicago, IL, 2020).

church (2 Tim. 1:14). Scripture does not say the man must be a world class evangelist-preacher. It simply says, 'able to teach,' or 'able to give instruction in sound doctrine and also to rebuke those who contradict it.' An elder must know and understand his Bible well enough to teach God's truths to God's people and to keep them from falling into error. He must be the kind of man that if you're struggling to understand something in the Scriptures or in your life, he will respond with a sound biblical answer.

The task of eldering is great and *carries heavy responsibility*. 1 Timothy 3:1 reads, 'If anyone aspires to the office of overseer, he desires a noble task.' Godly men should desire to be elders, but this aspiration shouldn't go unchecked. For James warns us in James 3:1, 'not many of you should become teachers, my brothers, for you know that we who teach will be judged with greater strictness.' No one should ever become an elder lightly. Hebrews 13:17 notes they are those 'who will have to give an account' for the souls over whom they keep watch. To desire the office of elder is to desire greater responsibility for the people in your care.

Finally, the office of elder is reserved for *qualified men only*. 1 Timothy 2:11-12 states, 'Let a woman learn quietly and with all submissiveness. I do not allow a woman to teach or to exercise authority over a man, she is to remain quiet.'[9] In these verses women are encouraged to learn but precluded from teaching men in the gathered assembly.[10] Paul grounds his commands in the creation order (vv. 13-14). God's design is for men to lead and women

---

9   See also 1 Cor. 14:33-34, 'As in all the churches of the saints, the women should keep silent in the churches.'

10   It's worth noting here that the emphasis of Paul's teaching here is actually that women are 'to learn' (v.11). Learn is the main Greek verb. That was a truly radical thought amongst Paul's Jewish contemporaries who did not approve of women studying the Torah. Women are to learn quietly with all submissiveness as opposed to teaching men. So the emphasis is what they are to do (learn), not just what they are not to do (teach, and in context, Paul means in the gathered assembly).

to follow their lead. That complementarity we see in the garden plays out here in the church. It is very clear in Titus 2 that God intends women to be teachers! But they are to teach other women. When it comes to women teaching in the gathered Sunday morning assembly, the question is not one of ability, but role. As women we are equal in value and dignity with men (Gen. 1:26-27), but different in role and function.[11] This means we have the privilege of using our 'femaleness' in a God-prescribed, God-glorifying way that beautifully demonstrates God's good design for women. We need theologically thoughtful, robust, strong, educated women serving and teaching within our churches. This is why a book series like this is geared towards women. We want women of the Word equipped to teach and train other women and the next generation of believers in theological truths.[12] So much more could be said on this issue, but for our purposes here I want us to see that according to the Scriptures, the office of elder is reserved for men alone.

SHEPHERDING THE FLOCK

A tender shepherd, a loving husband, a faithful father.[13] These are some of God's descriptions for Himself and how He relates to His people. The heart of God for His people is one of great love. He protects and provides for them. Elders are to be models of husbandly love for the bride, setting an example for them to follow. They do this when they gather and to guard the sheep entrusted to their care, feed them the Word of God, and equip them for the work of the ministry.

---

11 For further study see Claire Smith's, *God's Good Design: What the Bible Really Says about Men and Women* (London: The Good Book Company, 2012). Or Sharon James', *God's Design for Women in an age of gender confusion* (Durham: Evangelical Press, 2019).

12 Wilkin, Jen, *Women of the Word*, (Wheaton, IL; Crossway, 2014)

13 John 10:11-15, Isaiah 54:5, 2 Corinthians 6:18

The word 'shepherd' most thoroughly encompasses what elders are to do and be for God's people. They are first to gather and to guard the sheep entrusted to them. In the Old Testament the shepherds God placed over His people failed dreadfully at their tasks. Jeremiah 50:6 reads, 'My people have been lost sheep. Their shepherds have led them astray, turning them away on the mountains. From mountain to hill they have gone. They have forgotten their fold.' But God promises that He 'will bring them back to their fold, and they shall be fruitful and multiply. I will set shepherds over them who will care for them, and they shall fear no more, nor be dismayed, neither shall any be missing, declares the LORD' (Jer. 23:3-4). This is the ministry Jesus took up, gathering the sheep around His voice, and then guarding them so that none goes astray. Elders are to model this kind of protective, loving, servant-hearted leadership as under-shepherds of the chief shepherd Himself, Jesus Christ. Elders are to keep watch and to guard the flock, as we saw in Acts 20:28. Or consider 1 Peter 5:2-3 where the apostles writes to the elders, as a fellow elder, exhorting them to, 'shepherd the flock of God that is among you, exercising oversight, not under compulsion, but willingly, as God would have you; not for shameful gain, but eagerly; not domineering over those in your charge, but being examples to the flock.' This kind of steady, faithful leading takes patience, grace, and an inordinate amount of love and dedication to the task.

Elders gather and guard the sheep by feeding them the Word of God. The ministry of the Word and its primary role in the lives of the elders is imperative for them to fulfill the charge given to them by God. This is why in Acts 6 we see the apostles establishing the service role of deacon. They understood that, 'it is not right that we should give up preaching the word of God to serve tables...but we will devote ourselves to prayer and to ministry of the word' (Acts 6:2-4). The ministry of the Word must be first and foremost in the lives of elders. We know 'man does not live by bread alone, but by every word that proceeds from the mouth of God.'[14] God's very Word is the most important food we consume every day. As elders daily feed themselves the Word they are specifically tasked with feeding the sheep through the ministry of teaching and preaching. This concern for the Word should mark every elder, but it's also why some are specifically set aside for this task.[15] There will be some elders whose primary job responsibility is to prepare weekly sermons to feed God's Word to the hungry sheep. Pastor Joe Carter helpfully notes, 'The consistent testimony of the New Testament appears to be that Gospel ministers should make their living from Gospel work. Preaching is no man's hobby. It deserves the largest share of our time and attention and therefore it ought to be the means by which a Gospel worker supports himself and his family.'[16] The ministry of feeding the Word to the sheep through preaching and teaching is of primary importance. The question for you, reader, is whether or not you come to church each week ready to be fed.

Notice, too, how closely tied the preaching and teaching of the Word is with prayer (Acts 6:4). These two things must go hand in hand, for an elder cannot possibly understand the Word of God he is studying without the Spirit of God to illuminate it for him. Prayer is also how elders set an example of dependence upon God the sheep can follow. As we noted, overseers of the flock will give an account for each one of the sheep in their care. Only God has the power to protect the sheep, so praying for them individually, collectively, and corporately is another way the elders guard the sheep. In 1 Timothy 4:16 we read Paul warn Timothy to, 'keep a close watch on yourself and on the teaching. Persist in this, for by so doing you will save both yourself and your hearers.' Elders keep

---

14   Deuteronomy 8:3, Matthew 4:4

15   1 Timothy 5:17-18, 1 Corinthians 9:9-12

16   TGC Canadian edition, 'Should Pastors Be Paid,' January 9, 2019.

close watch on the sheep and on their teaching by submitting both to God in prayer.

Finally, we know from reading Ephesians 4:12 that the elders are 'to equip the saints for the work of ministry, for building up the body of Christ.' Elders themselves are not to be doing all the ministry, but training and equipping the saints for the ministry. They 'equip' by teaching and praying so that we, the members, can 'build up the body of Christ' to maturity (4:13). Elders prepare us for the one-anothering we'll discuss in chapter 8. They equip the body to build itself up in love (Eph. 4:16). Additionally, elders raise up and train other qualified men in the congregation to serve as elders. They entrust biblical teaching 'to faithful men, who will be able to teach others also' (2 Tim. 2:2). Elders should work to duplicate themselves, making disciples who can serve as elders, allowing the work of the shepherds to continue. In this way, the shepherds feed the sheep who do the work of ministry over generations in faithful churches.

God gives elders to shepherd the church as a means of grace and a gift to her. This is good authority that can be trusted. We saw the authority of the congregation and now we see the authority of elders. So now the question is: How should the congregation and the elders relate to one another?

Follow the leader

The relationship of the congregation to her pastors is one of balance between authority and mutual trust. When the members of a church see their pastors laying down their lives for their sake, they will be more apt to give themselves to those leaders. It's much like a godly marriage that is functioning well. A wife will happily follow her husband when she sees he has her best interests at heart and is willing to lay himself down for her as he leads. My husband has a tender heart and God gave him a strong woman to lead. After twenty-three years of marriage, we continue to grow in the dance of a godly complementarian home. The way he gently, but clearly directs and appeals to me instead of demanding and mandating has helped me grow in trust of his leadership in our marriage. He leads me by appealing with counsel, rarely with command. Our move to Arkansas was not an easy decision for this California girl, but Brad gently pursued my thoughts and feelings and urged me with God's Word to consider where God might be leading us. In the end, his loving leadership made following a delight, even though it wasn't always easy. Elders are to lead with that same disposition. They are to appeal with reason and wisdom, by the Word of God, to the congregation's sense of right and wrong and not simply lord their authority over them.

Paul demonstrated this well in Acts 17:10-12 when he encountered the curiosity and spiritual interests of the Bereans. Paul, an apostle, was not frustrated with their questions, but rather commended them, using his authority to encourage their searching of the Scriptures. The consequence was that many came to believe, including a number of prominent Greek women and men!

Elders have responsibility toward their congregations but congregations also have responsibilities toward their elders. God's Word clearly states that as much as the elders are to be respectable, the church is to respect and honor them. Paul instructs Timothy and the church at Ephesus, 'Let the elders who rule well be considered worthy of double honor, especially those who labor in preaching and teaching' (1 Tim. 5:17). The letter to the Hebrews teaches, 'Obey your leaders and submit to them, for they are keeping watch over your souls, as those who will have to give an account. Let them do this with joy and not with groaning, for that would be of no advantage to you' (13:17). The relationship of the congregation to her elders should bring joy and advantage as elders lead and members submit.

But when do we follow the leaders and when do we question? Two helpful categories to keep in mind are seriousness and clarity.[17] The more serious and clear an issue is, the more important it is for the church body to be involved. For example, if the gospel is clearly being denied by the senior or lead pastor, it is imperative that the church as a whole be involved because the matter is deadly serious and the situation is clear. The less clear but very serious matters are when trusting your elders is more difficult but most important. As men called to teach, your elders might decide on programming where teaching is planned and structured without bringing it to the church for a decision. But they would bring before the church the nomination of a new elder or a church-planting opportunity. All of these decisions require the congregation to trust her elders whether or not the decisions are brought up for a vote. It's good for the congregation to ask questions but we should check our hearts. Are we asking questions to get clarity and understanding or are we asking out of suspicion and cynicism? Do we want our way or do we desire to give way for the greater good. As Pastor Mark Dever has written, 'The congregation is not in competition with the elders. The congregation's authority is more like an emergency brake than a steering wheel. The congregation more normally recognizes than creates, responds rather than initiates, confirms rather than proposes.'[18] Our affirmation of elder leadership advantages us as we make their ministry a joy.

The congregation and the elders are to serve one another and depend upon God together for the glory of His name through the church. If you don't know your elders well or don't feel known by them, might I encourage you to reach out to connect with at

---

17   Denver, Mark; *Display of God's Glory*, (Washington D.C.: Nine Marks, 2019); p. 40-41 contains a helpful graph and description. I'm grateful to Mark Dever for teaching this concept in my membership class at Capitol Hill Baptist Church in 2000.

18   Dever, Mark, *The Church*, p. 143

least one? They want to know you. They are responsible for your soul. Leaders must be trustworthy and members must be capable of trusting. Rottenness creeps into the church when the leaders appear 'greasy' or when a congregation is suspicious of her leaders. Dever has helpfully said, 'It is a serious spiritual deficiency in a church either to have leaders who are untrustworthy, or members incapable of trusting.'[19] A church must either trust her leaders, replace them, or leave them for leaders they can trust. The thing members cannot do is say they affirm them, and then refuse to follow them.

Deacons

Service is the life of every Christian. As believers we are called to follow in the footsteps of the ultimate servant, our Lord Jesus Christ (Phil. 2:5-8). He came 'not to be served but to serve, and to give his life as a ransom for many' (Mark 10:45). Deacons are those specifically set aside to serve and strengthen the church. But exactly what are they? What do they do? Who should be deacons? Are they just elders in training?

God's Word speaks to us to help us better understand the nature, role, and function of deacons, beginning with their origin in Acts 6:

> Now in these days when the disciples were increasing in number, a complaint by the Hellenists arose against the Hebrews because their widows were being neglected in the daily distribution. And the twelve summoned the full number of the disciples and said, 'It is not right that we should give up preaching the word of God to serve tables. Therefore, brothers, pick out from among you seven men of good repute, full of the Spirit and of wisdom, whom we will appoint to this duty. But we will devote ourselves to prayer and to the ministry of the word.' And what they said pleased the whole gathering, and they chose

19 Dever, Mark; *Nine Marks of a Healthy Church*, (Crossway Books, 2004), p. 227

Stephen, a man full of faith and of the Holy Spirit, and Philip, and Prochorus, and Nicanor, and Timon, and Parmenas, and Nicolaus, a proselyte of Antioch. These they set before the apostles, and they prayed and laid their hands on them. And the word of God continued to increase, and the number of the disciples multiplied greatly in Jerusalem, and a great many of the priests became obedient to the faith (Acts 6:1-7).

The early church was prospering when a disagreement broke out about unequal treatment among the body of believers. The Greek-speaking Jewish widows were being neglected in the daily distribution of food. The solution was not to have the apostles neglect the preaching of the Word of God, but rather to set aside seven 'table waiters' or 'deacons' within the body. As we see in verse 4, this would allow the apostles to continue their *devotion to prayer* and the *ministry of the word* which is necessary for the church to survive and grow. This priority is what distinguishes the ministry of elders from that of deacons.

THE HEART OF A SERVANT

Servanthood is to mark all Christians, yet it must characterize those chosen for the office of deacon. That's the first mark of a godly deacon.[20] He or she must have a servant's heart. In Acts 6, some of the Hellenistic widows were literally forgotten (or intentionally neglected) when the food was distributed! Instead of hiring a staff

---

20   The qualifications for deacons are set forth in 1 Timothy 3:8-13. They are much the same as elders, except they aren't required to be able to teach, and there is no prohibition on women filling the office as biblically defined. If you'd like to think more about this topic, see Appendix 1 of Matt Smethurst's book, *Deacons: How they Serve and Strengthen the Church* (Wheaton, IL: Crossway, 2021). It helpfully spells out the arguments for and against women deacons. See also Mark Dever's note on page 7 of *The Church Basics: Understanding Church Leadership*, (Nashville, TN: B&H publishing, 2016).

member or establishing a task-force, the congregation sets aside seven qualified men to meet these physical and administrative needs

The word 'deacon' occurs as a noun or verb three times in this passage. At its root, 'to deacon' is 'to serve.' For many cultures today, however, service is seen as menial and is often undervalued. Leadership, production, strength, and authority, that's what we value. Consider the last time you went out to eat. Your server played an integral part in you receiving and enjoying the meal prepared for you. Most likely you showed some level of kindness and graciousness to them as they waited on you, caring for your needs. Now imagine Julia Child, one of the most prominent chefs of all time, walking out from the kitchen during that most delightful meal. Would you greet her with the same kindness and graciousness as your server, or with greater deference and respect? Chances are you might be tempted to jump up to try and grab a selfie with her! Culturally, we are trained to see Julia Child as more deserving of admiration and value. But if Ms. Child spent the time serving, cleaning, arranging and distributing food she would not have the time necessary to do the hard work of preparing and cooking the meal. The servers and wait staff assist in the physical and administrative part of running a restaurant so that the chef is freed to give herself to her work.

It's important for us to note that the Bible upends these cultural values. Jesus Himself saw servanthood very differently than the world. John 12:26 says, 'If anyone serves (deacons) me, he must follow me; and where I am, there will my servant (deacon) be also.' Or in Matthew 20:26, 'But whoever would be great among you must be your servant (deacon).' In Acts 6:4 the apostles are said to be devoted to 'ministry' of the Word and prayer. That Word ministry is related to service. But in order to give themselves to the service of the Word and prayer for others they needed the help of other servants. Deacons are chosen to serve those who are themselves serving the Word.

Protect the Quarterback

I grew up in a household of athletic boys and now we live in an SEC football city where fall game days are an epic event. So when I read Matt Smethurst's analogy for deacons I immediately resonated. He writes, 'Biblical deacons are like a congregation's offensive linemen, whose job is to protect the quarterback. They rarely get attention, much less credit, but their labors are utterly indispensable for both guarding and advancing the ministry of the Word. Without effective deacons, elders will suffer incessant distraction and get sacked by an onrush of practical demands.'[21] Yes! Invaluable and often unseen describes a deacon well.

Meeting both the physical and administrative needs of a church requires both a proactive and reactive response. It's a matter of responding to difficulties and demands in real time, but also anticipating future needs and possible problems. In doing so, deacons support the elders and build up the church. Their practical service pours over into their supportive service. Since deacons come alongside the elders in their ministry, having clearly defined duties and areas of focus aids the church more than having a myriad of people serving with ill-defined roles. For example, a church could have a deacon of ordinances or parking or hospitality or greeting or weddings. You get the picture. This does *not* mean the deacon does all the work in his or her specified area, but he or she should organize and coordinate that particular work for the church body.

Key to the role of any deacon is to promote the spiritual unity of the body. Now this ought to be the concern of all Christians,[22] but particularly for those set aside by the church as deacons. This concern for unity guided Acts 6 and is the reason deacons should be 'full of the Spirit and of wisdom' (v. 3). Deacons should be those

---

21   Smethurst, Matt, *Deacons*, p. 75. For a fuller and more comprehensive treatment of the topic of deacons, this book is an invaluable resource.

22   Ephesians 4:3, 13 & 1 Peter 3:8

excited about building up the body of believers and anxious to do it, more than desiring recognition for it. Pastor Thabiti Anyabwile notes, 'A solid deacon prioritizes God over man, the soul over the body, and eternity over time even while he attends to the important practical and bodily needs of the people.'[23] (As a mother of four, this sounds very similar to the role of a godly wife and mother.)

A deacon's goal of meeting needs should be the edification of the church, not the exaltation of self. Practically, this means deacons shouldn't be territorial about, or frustrated with, others 'interfering' with their area of focus. It also means it isn't wise to have deacons who are dissatisfied with the church. No church is perfect, but *if a deacon sees the church's faults and failures before they see Christ's work in her, they won't serve well.* Deacons are like the suspension in a car. They're meant to absorb the shocks and bumps for a smooth ride, not accentuate them.[24] Godly deacons tend to be unseen but vitally important for the stability of the church, just like properly operating shocks for your car.

Avoiding chaos

A world without authority is chaos and anarchy. We need good leaders and thoughtful, obedient followers. In the Godhead we see the beauty of headship and authority perfectly executed between the Father and the Son and the Holy Spirit in the creation of this world and the salvation of sinners. God created His church to function with that same good authority! In 1 Corinthians 14:40, Paul concludes a passage on the church gathering with these words, 'But all things should be done decently and in order.' For as he states in verse 33 of that chapter, 'For God is not a God of confusion but of peace.' God is not about chaos when it comes to His church. He desires things to be done in an orderly way.

---

23   Anyabwile, Thabiti, *Finding Faithful Elders & Deacons*, (Crossway, 2012), p. 25

24   Smethurst, Matt, *Deacons*, p. 54

In the words of Bobby Jamieson, 'A church is born when gospel people form a gospel polity [government].' [25] It's one thing for a group of believers to gather 'in the name of Jesus,' assuming that constitutes a true church, but as we've seen, the Bible has a different description. One of the big differences between a random group of Christians who meet in the grocery store aisle and a church is polity! When all is going well in a church, polity won't seem to matter. It's when things go sideways, that polity pops into video color and makes all the difference in the world. [26]

25   Jamieson, B, *Going Public: Why Baptism is Required for Church Membership* (Nashville, TN: B&H Academic, 2015)

26   See introduction to this book for a practical application of this point

QUESTIONS

'A FLOCK WITH A JOB TO DO: CONGREGATIONALISM, ELDERS, AND DEACONS'

How churches choose to arrange themselves isn't just a random process. The Bible gives specific roles and organizational structures. Elder-led congregationalism is the biblical authority structure of the church used to guard the gospel of Christ.

1. What job did Jesus give the church to do?

2. What are four things members of churches are to exercise authority over?

3. What is an elder?

4. Who can serve as an elder, and what are the qualifications to serve?

5. How are your elders gifts to you?

6. Read and consider the qualifications for elders and deacons in 1 Timothy 3:1-13. What stands out to you?

7. In what ways do you take your responsibilities as a member of your church seriously? How do you treat members' meetings?

8. Do you know the elders of your church? How do you pray for the elders of your church? How do you affirm their leadership and seek to understand when things are unclear?

9. If you are frustrated with the leadership in your church have you considered how you might be able to better know them so you might grow in trust of them?

10. If you have deacons in your church, how do you encourage them? Though not in it for the accolades, every Christian needs encouragement from brothers and sisters in Christ!

Chapter 8

A Different Kind of Community:
Life With One Another

We will feast in the house of Zion
We will sing with our hearts restored
He has done great things, we will say together
We will feast and weep no more
We will not be burned by the fire
He is the Lord, our God.
We are not consumed by the flood
Upheld, protected, gathered up

'We Will Feast in the House of Zion'
Sandra McCracken

An ad campaign for Facebook groups touts, 'something for everyone.' These virtual 'communities' are formed with people that have any number of shared interests, hobbies, histories, cultures, ethnicities, activities, and more. Community is a buzzword these days. People are looking to connect with others for friendship, relationships, and camaraderie. My husband and I are a part of an early morning adult swim group. Over time the other participants moved from merely fellow swim enthusiasts to new friends. Our shared interest was a gateway to forming new relationships. This can happen in almost any scenario: soccer moms from the same traveling team, volunteers in a crisis pregnancy clinic, knitting clubs, regulars at the Tuesday/Thursday morning Orange Theory, hiking clubs, book clubs, etc. We like to make connections based upon commonalities and shared interests and allow those to be the foundation upon which to build community. Part of that longing and desire is a God-given reality. We weren't created to be alone. We were created to be a part of a community – something bigger, something beyond us. As Christians, we understand this community to be the church, which God is building through the gospel.

Because Christians understand the desire for community is given to us by a loving God,[1] we ought to see church relationships through different lenses. Our connection is *spiritual*, not merely physical, relational, social, or shared interests. In Christ, we have a commonality that transcends those earthly realities. It is not of this world. In fact, as redeemed members of God's new community, we may have virtually nothing in common from a worldly perspective, but we have everything in common from a heavenly one. The local church is the place where that heavenly community is displayed, and where Jesus Christ is raised up as the central figure we all have in common. That means our worldly diversity ought to be a marker of our spiritual unity in Christ.[2]

You might be scratching your head and wondering exactly how this whole 'church' thing works together. In this chapter we are going to look at what it is to do 'life together' in a local church and practice that kind of unique community I just described. We get to talk about what it looks like to be in God's family, as God designed. For in Romans 12 and 1 Corinthians 12, Paul uses the

---

1   Genesis 2:18, 17:7, Exodus 6:7, Ezekiel 34:30-31, Jeremiah 31:33, 1
    Peter 2:9-10, are just a few examples.

2   For more on this point of unity in diversity, see chapter 6

image of one body with many members, each member being indispensable for the proper functioning of the body (Rom. 12:3-8; 1 Cor. 12:12-26). How those individual members are to function together is captured in the many 'one-another,' commands of the New Testament. In fact, the Greek word commonly translated into English as 'one another' or 'each other' is used 100 times in the New Testament and over half are used in letters directed specifically to churches. As individual Christians, we cannot possibly obey all of the New Testament's commands by living our lives alone and apart from other believers in a local church because they are *'one another'* commands. They can't be met with an individualistic mentality. They require us to belong to, to be integrated into, and to commit to a specific, local body of believers.

What's worth noting is how often 'one another' is used throughout the New Testament and what that means for us today living lives as Christians under the new covenant. As wonderful as it would be to go through and consider each and every 'one another' command, I've chosen to focus on the most emphasized verses that most directly relate to our corporate life together. Let's turn now and consider what it looks like for us, as a family in Christ, to, as Paul said to the church at Philippi, conduct ourselves in a manner worthy of the gospel, standing firm together in one spirit and striving side by side for the faith of the gospel, 'living in harmony with one another in accord with Christ Jesus.'[3]

What's love got to do with it? Everything!

There are all kinds of conversations around 'love.' Questions like, 'What makes you feel loved? Do you know your love language?' Yard Signs scream with indignity, 'Love is love.' Graffiti declares, 'Love, not Hate!' But what does it mean to love someone? I've been married for twenty-three years now and I feel like I'm just beginning to understand the concept of truly loving another

3   Philippians 1:27, Romans 15:5

person. True love is others-oriented. There are various kinds of love, but they all require commitment and resolve, a 'looking out' for someone else's interests above and beyond your own. God tells us in His Word to, 'walk in love, as Christ loved us and gave himself up for us.'[4] Love for one another encompasses all the other 'one-another's' we are going to consider, which is why it is our starting point. It's our foundation for how to do life together as members of local churches. Like the root system for a beautiful peony bush, so love nurtures and feeds the blossoms of our one-anothering. If we 'have not love, we are nothing.'[5] This is where Jesus begins.

In John 13, Jesus predicts His betrayal by one of His own. As soon as this disciple, Judas, departs from the group Jesus turns to the remaining disciples and says these words to them, 'A new commandment I give to you that you love one another: just as I have loved you, you also are to love one another. By this, all people will know that you are my disciples, if you have love for one another.'[6] John is contrasting Judas' betrayal and abandonment against the kind of love the disciples are to display. Jesus is calling them to show their love for Him in how they love one another. Just as Jesus will demonstrate His love for these disciples through His suffering and death, He calls them to love one another willingly, sacrificially, universally, and earnestly.[7] It's why Paul exhorts the Colossians in a list of attributes they should be striving for, that 'above all these put on love, which binds everything together in perfect harmony.'[8] The principal duty we have in the church is to love one another. Our mutual love is the proof that we are disciples of Christ.

4   Ephesians 5:2

5   Paraphrase of 1 Corinthians 13:2

6   John 13:34-35

7   Romans 13:8, 1:15, 1 Peter 1:22, 2:17, 3:8, 4:8

8   Colossians 3:14

A New Kind of Family

The love for one another that Jesus expects is a familial kind of love. In Christ we are brought into a new family. We are a family of believers, bought by the blood of Jesus. Our bloodline flows through Christ to us, knitting our hearts together supernaturally. We, who would have been enemies, are now brothers and sisters in Christ. Although He had biological relationships, Jesus emphasized the priority of spiritual relationships as our true, eternal family. When teaching and ministering to the crowds one day His family sought to speak with Him, but His reply was simply, 'Who is my mother, and who are my brothers?' Motioning to the crowd He exclaimed, ' Here are my mother and my brothers! For whoever does the will of my Father in heaven is my brother and sister and mother' (Matt. 12:48-50). Luke 14:26 records one of the most shocking statements Jesus makes about the cost of following Him. He said, 'If anyone comes to me and does not hate his own father and mother and wife and children and brothers and sisters, yes, and even his own life, he cannot be my disciple.' His statement in no way discounts or nullifies the importance of loving our biological family and honoring our parents. Jesus' comment is shocking because it redefines our understanding of true family. Even on the cross, Jesus looked out to His mother and His disciple standing nearby and said, '"Woman behold, your son!" Then he said to the disciple, "Behold, your mother!" And from that hour the disciple took her to his own home.'[9] Right here we see Jesus defining the love we are to have within the Christian community. It is to be a love like that of family.

In Paul's first pastoral letter to Timothy, whom he calls his 'true child in the faith.' he talks about this familial love and relationship that is to mark the church. He writes, 'Do not rebuke an older man, but exhort him as a father, younger men as brothers, older

---

9   John 19:26-27

women as mothers and younger women as sisters with all purity.'[10] This exhortation does not discount our biological relationships, it redefines all of our relationships from the perspective of eternity. When my oldest daughter, Page, was baptized and brought into the membership of our church, she became my sister in Christ in addition to being my biological daughter. In effect, our relationship was enhanced! Our temporal earthly relationship was now one that will span for all eternity. What a sweet thought for this mama's heart! Theologian, Edmund Clowney states it this way, 'Christians in community must again show the world, not merely family values, but the bond of the love of Christ.'[11]

According to Paul in Romans 12:10, we are to 'Love one another with a brotherly affection. Outdo one another in showing honor,' and in Philippians 2:4, 'Let each of you look not only to his own interest, but also to the interests of others.' Our hearts and eyes should be set on things above and not on earthly things, and this includes how we love and care for the spiritual family we will spend eternity with in heaven. That's what the supernatural love of Christ looks like in the life of a believer.

I came back to the hospital last night after I finished a shift on the floor because Heather, my friend and sister in Christ from our church, was delivering her baby. Due to this prolonged Covid season many women have not been able to have their mothers or other support people with them. As part of their spiritual family, I have the unique privilege of coming alongside these sisters. What struck me was the surprise from my coworkers that after working almost thirteen straight hours I would come back to support and encourage her, unpaid! As I walked down the hall to her room, two of my fellow nurses inquired, 'Are you a friend from her church? Is that why you came back?' I smiled and nodded, thankful for another opportunity to show the world not merely biological family, but

10   1 Timothy 5:1, CSB

11   Clowney, Edmund, *The Church*, (IVP, 1995), p. 16

spiritual family. With almost twenty years of age between us, it didn't look like a 'normal' kind of friendship deserving that kind of sacrifice. (I'm old enough to be her mother!) But our shared spiritual family draws our hearts together to demonstrate a different kind of love the world is not used to seeing.

When God saves us He puts a new heart in us, changing our affections and desires. We no longer look to shared interests, hobbies, careers, or even ethnicities to bind us to other Christians. We share the most important commonality of all time, Christ Himself! We have more in common with those who are outwardly 'opposite' of us if they are in Christ, than we do with those outside of Christ, with whom we share many earthly commonalities. You could expound on the old adage and say, 'Christ's shared blood is thicker than water.' This is why churches that specialize their services for a certain demographic actually harm the gospel witness. Love across age, gender and cultural boundary lines preaches the gospel loudly to the world. What doesn't make sense to the world can only make sense in Christ. That is the others-oriented, radical kind of love that God calls us to in Christ. This love is the foundation of our life together in Christ.

Crossbeams of Support: bearing with one another

So what does this familial love look like lived out in our everyday lives? First, it looks like bearing with one another. Our love for one another spills over into many other areas of life together. Ephesians 4:1-2 tells us to 'walk in a manner worthy of the calling to which you have been called, with all humility and gentleness, with patience, *bearing with one another in love*' (emphasis mine). In the previous verse Paul is praying for God's glory to be manifested in the church.[12] His glory is manifested through the lives of His people and their unity together. This includes bearing with one another in love. What does it mean to bear with someone? To bear

---

12   Ephesians 3:21

is to support or hold something up. Much like a cross beam holds up the weight of a ceiling, we are to support each other. Bearing implies a kind of endurance. A crossbeam holds up the ceiling for the duration of the house. Brothers and sisters in Christ support each other without giving up.

As Christians, we are called to bear with our brothers' and sisters' differences, weaknesses and even sin. Differences manifest themselves in any number of ways. Unique personality quirks, eccentricities, individual dispositions, or even cultural differences can feel challenging to love. But the truth is that what can be strange to us is often normal to others and vice versa! In God's grand design He made us male and female, in His image, with a variety of looks, personalities and gifts. Diversity in the church displays God's glory. The 'manifold wisdom of God' is made known through the church (Eph. 3:10) as we bear with brothers and sisters who are different from us. Looking like a motley crew to the world is a benefit! Strangeness is to be embraced, not eschewed. When you gather with the saints this next week, consider who you gravitate towards and why. Do they look like you? Think like you? Act like you? Dress like you? Same age as you? It's worth noting here that the etymology of the word *hospitality* means 'lover of strangers.' So when we love others who are 'strange' to us, we practice radical, God-glorifying hospitality. Might I encourage you to reach out to those who seem 'strange' or different from you? You may not have anything in common from the outside looking in, but you do have the most important thing, Jesus! Backing up from that passage we considered in Colossians 3, Paul says in verses 10-11, 'put on the new self, which is being renewed in knowledge after the image of its creator. Here there is not Greek and Jew, circumcised and uncircumcised, barbarian, Scythian, slave, free; but Christ is all, and in all.' That dividing wall of hostility was torn down in Christ, making us one body, members of the same household, and fellow citizens with the saints.[13] The world's idea of similarity should not prove to be a barrier to our unity and fellowship as we bear with one another's strangeness and uniquenesses.

We also demonstrate our familial love for one another by bearing with one another's weaknesses. I'm not talking about how much you can bench or squat, but strength of character and perseverance in the Christian life. Christian maturity doesn't happen overnight. As I said yesterday morning to a dear friend struggling with her own limitations, 'you aren't what you once were and you're not what you will one day be, but rest assured that He is at work within you.' In the same way we don't expect a newborn to start walking at six weeks of age, we shouldn't expect a brand new believer to have answers to every Christian dilemma they encounter in their lives. They need other, stronger, more mature believers to come alongside them and walk with them and teach them how to think 'Christianly.' Paul understood this when he wrote, 'As for the one who is weak in faith, welcome him, but not to quarrel over opinions' (Rom. 14:1). He went on to underscore this in 15:1 with these words, 'We who are strong have an obligation to bear the failings of the weak,[14] and not to please ourselves.' We forbear with one another because we understand we have the most important thing in common and we share the same enemy. Jude writes in 22-23 (CSB), 'have mercy on those who waver, save others by snatching them from the fire.' Even the theologically particular Dr. Martyn Lloyd-Jones helpfully states, 'We must not be too particular in regard to what we believe, but we must have the spirit of fellowship and of friendship and of working together against the common enemy.'[15]

Lastly, and most importantly, we demonstrate the supernatural love of Christ when we bear with others when they sin against us.

---

13   Ephesians 2:14, 19

14   or 'weaknesses of those without strength' CSB

15   Lloyd-Jones, Dr Martyn, *Christian Unity: An Exposition of 4:1-16* (Nashville, TN: Baker Book House, 1981), p. 37

God calls us to forgive one another and be restored to unity as members of the household of God. In Colossians 3, we see the call for, 'bearing with one another and, if one has a complaint against another, forgiving each other as the Lord has forgiven you, so you also must forgive' (v. 13). Christ, the perfect, sinless, Son of God, has taken our sin upon Himself, bearing the full weight of God's wrath against those sins, clearing the way for us to know and receive full forgiveness from Him. Jesus' blood shed for us has set us free. We are completely and totally forgiven the moment we repent and believe. It is an astounding truth to consider. Every sin of ours was laid on Him. The same is true of our brothers and sisters in Christ. They have experienced the same radical forgiveness by God as well. There is no way to justify our unwillingness to extend or seek forgiveness from one another. Jesus said in Luke 7:47, 'But he who is forgiven little, loves little.' The opposite of that statement is equally true. The one who has been forgiven much, loves much, and 'love covers a multitude of sins' (1 Pet. 4:8).

The front page of the newspaper tells us about church shootings or when a pastor has a moral failing; but sadly, when forgiveness and restoration has occurred, it never makes the headlines. A number of years ago a very dear brother in Christ said some false things about me. I felt gutted when the rumors came to my ears. But what was remarkable was how quickly he came to seek my forgiveness and be reconciled. Even though I had been wounded deeply, the result was a dramatic increase in our love and affection for one another. A lot of time has passed since that day, but his urgency to be restored was so encouraging it feels like it happened yesterday. The conflict served to strengthen our love for one another and demonstrate our supernatural bond in Christ to others who were aware of the situation. If only those kinds of stories could hit the front page.

An Unbreakable Chain

Learning to bear with one another in love is a gift of grace to us from our Heavenly Father. He knows what we need before we even ask and He cares deeply for the reputation of His own name through His people. For the Apostle Paul this looked like giving up preferences for the sake of others. For us it might look like learning to bear with particular music choices in our weekly gatherings. It could also mean learning to bear with others in their political or educational choices. Things that people might divide relationships over outside the church don't necessarily need to divide us inside the church.

In his classic work, *Life Together,* Dietrich Bonhoeffer writes, 'In a Christian community everything depends upon whether each individual is an indispensable link in a chain. Only when even the smallest link is securely interlocked is the chain unbreakable... Every Christian community must realize that not only do the weak need the strong, but also that the strong cannot exist without the weak. The elimination of the weak is the death of fellowship.'[16] In 1 Corinthians 12, Paul spells out the need for every part of the body, as those parts work for the common good of the whole. As church members it is our responsibility to strive for this kind of unity as we bear with one another in love. It's our privilege to carry each other's burdens and sorrows,[17] forgive and be forgiven, cross barriers, and be united together, bearing with one another in love for the sake of our gospel witness.

Providers, not consumers: serving one another

The Christian life is a life of service. Jesus' very words to His disciples in Mark 10:45 were, 'For even the Son of Man came not to be served but to serve, and to give his life as a ransom for many.' Jesus came to this earth in order to live the life we could not live,

16   Bonhoeffer, Dietrich, *Life Together* (Harper & Row, 1954), p. 94.

17   Galatians 1:1-2

die the death we deserved, and to rise again, securing salvation for all those who would turn from their sins and put their trust in Him. While He lived among us, He spoke often about denying ourselves, taking up our cross, and following Him.[18] His suffering was an act of service for His people and as His people we are called to follow in the footsteps of our Savior. 1 Peter 2:21 says, 'For to this you have been called, because Christ also suffered for you, leaving you an example so that you might follow in his steps.' To love Jesus is to love His people. To obey Jesus is to follow in His footsteps of surrendering ourselves for the good of one another.

The book of 1 John centers around this idea of love for one another through service. It's a 'love in action' kind of love. John writes in 3:16-18, 'By this we know love, that he laid down his life for us, and we ought to lay down our lives for the brothers. But if anyone has the world's goods and sees his brother in need, yet closes his heart against him, how does God's love abide in him? Little children, let us not love in word or talk but in deed and in truth.' We are called to lay down our lives for others just as Jesus laid down His life for us.

We began training our children to be 'helpers' when they were very little. As soon as they could walk, we would change their diapers and have them throw the dirty ones in the trash for us. Even at that young age, they found joy in being able to 'help mommy (or daddy)' and serve in that small way. Being a member of the church is to be a part of a family. And being part of being a family is to contribute to the welfare of the home. We are called to be providers and not just consumers. John Calvin says, 'Scripture warns us that whatever we have freely received from the Lord is given to us on the condition that it be used for the common good of the church.'[19] The amount we need to consume or are able to provide will vary

---

18 Matthew 16:24, Luke 9:23.

19 Calvin, John; *The Little Book on the Christian Life*, (Reformation Trust, 2017); p. 36

with the seasons and circumstances of our lives, but our eye should always be toward service, even in our weakness.[20]

When teaching about spiritual gifts, Paul exhorted the church at Corinth to 'strive to excel in building up the church.' We should use all of our gifts to build up the church. That means we should initiate involvement in each other's lives to be built up in the things of the Lord. We serve by spurring others on toward the love and good deeds[21] that God has prepared in advance for them to do.[22] And as we build up and into one another, our foundational goal to love one another is bolstered. Love and service go hand in hand. We established in chapter 3, in looking at Jesus' departing words to His disciples in Matthew 28:19-20, that the primary mission of the church is to make disciples. We serve others by pouring our lives into them to make disciples. How do we do that? Imitation is a fact of life in the local church. We are to be living our lives in such a way that we can say with Paul, 'follow me as I follow Christ.'[23] 1 Thessalonians underscores the importance of living this kind of replicable life among one another. The believers in Thessalonica imitated Christ. They also imitated the apostles and previously established churches. In turn, they became examples to others (1:6 and 2:14). We promote the holiness of God's people when we get involved in each other's lives and say, 'Come follow me as I follow Jesus on our way home to heaven.' It's how we are called to serve one another as unto the Lord.

I grew up in a household full of boys. There wasn't always the verbal affirmation of love, but there was certainly the understanding that we were united as a family. No matter what was going on in our lives, if there was any need, someone would be there to meet it. We watched out for one another, had each other's backs, and

20   2 Corinthians 12:9

21   Hebrews 10:24

22   Ephesians 2:10

23   1 Corinthians 11:1

pushed one another along in life. I always knew how my brothers felt about my friends and whatever guy I was dating at the time. They served me in how they cared for and watched over me. That's what a family is supposed to do. Sadly, for many believers today they haven't known that kind of support in their own biological families. Their families may have even been places of violence and neglect. The church should be the place where we see God's design for the family. It's a place where we all come together to serve and in doing so are then served ourselves. We watch out for one another. God created the church family to demonstrate to the world, and to those with a warped and misguided view of family, the beauty of familial love. Each in service for the other. All for the glory of God.

More than just food: show hospitality to one another

Have you ever considered that momentous and memorable events transpire around food? Treaties are signed, marriages are celebrated, friends unite, all around a table with food. Most of us know this to be true, but the reality is, hospitality takes time and effort. Sometimes it's inconvenient and awkward. In the book of 1 Peter he writes to suffering Christians, reminding them that the end of all things is at hand and, then turns around, telling them to practice hospitality.[24] Peter knows that hospitality is difficult, which is why he tags on a modifier at the end of the sentence, 'without grumbling.' He knows the challenge of being truly hospitable.

Hospitality is intentionally opening up our homes and our hearts to others. As I noted earlier, the word itself means 'lover of strangers.' It's not just some kind of a 'holy huddle' or 'hanging together' so we can 'love on each other.' It is a deliberate and intentional act of serving and loving our brothers and sisters in Christ so we can put all those other 'one-anothers' into practice. It takes preparation and foresight. It takes sacrifice and a commitment of time and money, but the fruit is sweet! It's the kind of gathering

---

24   1 Peter 4:9

where, if we took all the commonalities away and the only thing left was Jesus, we'd have an amazing time together.

We love to invite a cross section of people over to our house after our morning worship service. Singles, families, older, younger, male, female, and any other variant we can add. It may feel a bit awkward for some, but they leave encouraged and built up simply by being in our home, getting to know their church family a little bit more.

The more we know one another, the better we are at doing intentional spiritual good in each other's lives. So when you do hospitality, ask about each other's conversion stories. If you have children, encourage them to sit and listen to what God has done in the lives of these spiritual family members they may not yet know. God just might use a 'stranger's' testimony to bring your child to repentance and faith! When appropriate, talk about sin struggles or family dynamics, work challenges, Bible study habits, or prayer patterns. There is so much we can learn from one another. We can act as iron sharpening iron, spurring one another on towards those love and good deeds. The dinner table is an incredible place of ministry!

Hospitality can be a structured time over a meal or dessert, so long as the goal is to welcome the stranger to the table as a means of growing in love and unity for the glory of God. But it isn't just the opening of the home and the dinner table where we practice hospitality. It's the opening of our lives and sharing ourselves: our time, our food, our homes, our prayers, our love. Hospitality can be as simple as inviting a sister to join you in your everyday life, folding laundry, doing dishes, working in the yard, or changing diapers. Rosaria Butterfield calls all of this 'radically ordinary' hospitality. She winsomely states, 'Those who live out radically ordinary hospitality see their homes not as theirs at all but as God's gift to use for the furtherance of his kingdom.'[25]

In 1 Thessalonians 2:8 when Paul is encouraging the church at Thessalonica, he talks about this very act of giving our lives away to one another. He writes, 'We cared so much for you that we were pleased to share with you not only the gospel of God, but also our own lives, because you had become dear to us' (CSB). It was a love so deep, he shared his very life with them and even refers to them as his 'joy and hope,' his 'crown of boasting'[26] That sounds like radical hospitality! He opened himself up and inconvenienced himself because of the love he had for them. Do you inconvenience yourself for your brothers and sisters in Christ? This is another way Jesus is an example for us to follow. He cares for strangers. He gave His life for us while we were still His enemies. He calls us to lose our life for His sake in order to gain our lives back. When we practice hospitality and earnestly strive to do intentional spiritual good in the lives of others, it glorifies our Lord Jesus as we follow in His footsteps, and we will find that any conveniences we have given up for the sake of hospitality will be well worth what we gain in return.

Submission is not a dirty word: Submit to one another

Submission has become such a dirty word. Filled with thoughts or memories of misuse of authority and even abuse, we fear to use the word in polite company. But the truth is that submission is a biblical word and a biblical idea; and, therefore, a beautiful one! As with so much of God's perfect creation, human sinfulness has distorted it, marring the picture it was meant to display. Submission is deeply embedded in the creation story. From the beginning God established an authority structure where headship and submission

---

25 Butterfield, Rosaria; *The Gospel Comes with a House Key*; (Crossway; 2018), p. 11

26 1 Thessalonians 2:19

played a role. Creation order speaks to God's good design for the home, workplace, nature, church, and even society. Much could be said on this topic,[27] but in the interest of focusing on God's call for submission within the church we'll zero in there.

In the book of Ephesians, Paul walks his readers through a glorious description of the gospel and how it should be lived out among God's people. In chapter 5 he exhorts them to be imitators of God, giving themselves up for one another, 'submitting to one another out of reverence for Christ.'[28] In the very next verse he commands wives to submit to their own husbands. If we're not careful readers we might be prone to think Paul made a mistake here and surely did not intend to call wives to submit to their own husbands after calling them to submit to one another. But context is our friend. As we continue to read we watch Paul lay out his argument in 5:22-6:9 by highlighting three types of relationships under authority: husbands and wives, children and parents, as well as slaves and masters. Ephesians 5:21 is calling readers to submit to one another as unto the Lord in their respective sphere, and so keep the created order God established back in the Garden of Eden. We are all under some kind of authority in our lives. God has called us to demonstrate the gospel in how we appropriately submit to authority structures we have in our lives. This demonstrates a love for one another and for the Lord God.

In the concluding section of the book of Hebrews, the writer commands the reader to, 'Obey your leaders and submit to them, for they are keeping watch over your souls, as those who will have to give an account. Let them do this with joy and not with groaning,

---

27 There are several excellent resources on this topic, but I would highly recommend Claire Smith's, *God's Good Design: What the Bible Really Says about Men and Women*. Or Sharon James', *God's Design for Women in an age of gender confusion*.

28 Ephesians 5:22

for that would be of no advantage to you.'[29] In the church, God has given elders to lead and to guide the particular group of God's people in that one local church. They are invested with authority given from God as under-shepherds of the chief shepherd, the Lord Jesus Christ.

Just as wives are to submit to their *own* husbands, so we, as church members, are called to submit to our elders. As members of a local church we are called to follow that example of submission as unto the Lord when we joyfully and lovingly follow their leadership. Paul wrote these words to the church at Thessalonica, 'We ask you, brothers, to respect those who labor among you and are over you in the Lord and admonish you, and to esteem them very highly in love because of their work. Be at peace among yourselves.'[30] Numerous times in the New Testament epistles there is a call to 'show regard' or 'recognition,' to 'give honor' to the leaders and teachers given to us by God.[31] This means we listen well to their teaching, obey their scriptural admonitions, follow their wise biblical counsel, and encourage and pray for them.

Our obedience and submission to our leaders brings them joy in their labors as they strive to guide and guard us, teaching and strengthening us by the Word of God as we walk the road together to heaven. My former pastor, Mark Dever, loved to quote this section from Charles Spurgeon to describe the role he had alongside the elders in caring for the sheep entrusted to their care. It's a fitting description of the sacrifice and heart of a true shepherd and the role we play in our life together:

> I am occupied in my small way, as Mr. Great-heart was employed in Bunyan's day. I do not compare myself with that champion, but I am in the same line of business. I am engaged

---

29   Hebrews 13:17

30   1 Thessalonians 5:12-13

31   Hebrews 13:7,17; Philippians 2:29; 1 Corinthians 16:16, 18.

in personally-conducted tours to Heaven; and I have with me, at the present time, dear Old Father Honest: I am glad he is still alive and active. And there is Christiana, and there are her children. It is my business, as best I can, to kill dragons, and cut off giants' heads, and lead on the timid and trembling. I am often afraid of losing some of the weaklings. I have the heart-ache for them; but, by God's grace, ***and your kind and generous help in looking after one another***, I hope we shall all travel safely to the river's edge. Oh, how many have I had to part with there! I have stood on the brink, and I have heard them singing in the midst of the stream, and I have almost seen the shining ones lead them up the hill, and through the gates, into the Celestial City.[32]

Mr. Spurgeon understood the gravity of the task given to him by God and thanked those in his care for how they cared for one another alongside him in the work. Let us pursue a life of submission to those in authority over us, blessing and encouraging them in their labors to lead us in the Lord as we seek to look after one another. They make sacrifices and carry burdens to the shepherd and lead the sheep. We should inconvenience ourselves to encourage them, showing them honor, and reminding them that their labor in the Lord is not in vain.[33]

Powerlessness: Don't neglect to pray for one another

Prayerless Christianity is powerless Christianity. In James 5:16 we are commanded to, 'confess your sins to one another and pray for one another, that you may be healed. The prayer of a righteous person has great power as it is working.' Prayer is not an option. It isn't something we can excuse ourselves out of because we're busy or our mind wanders or we're too shy to pray in front of people.

---

32 C.H. Spurgeon, *Autobiography*, vol. 2 (London: Passmore & Alabaster, 1898), p. 131. No modern reprint with this quotation is yet available.

33 1 Corinthians 15:58. See chapter 7 for more on elders.

We demonstrate our dependence upon God and our love for each other by praying for and with one another.

As the people of God, we have been given the gift of prayer. Because of Christ's atoning death on our behalf, the Holy Spirit literally indwells us, and the Father bids us come, pray. 'Come let's worship and bow down; let's kneel before the Lord, our Maker. For he is our God, and we are the people of his pasture, the sheep under his care.'[34] Our ability to pray is a gift from the triune God: The Father calls, the Son enables, and the Spirit intercedes. What an incredible privilege to come and pray to the Almighty God, the creator and sustainer of all life. We have unhindered access to His throne, His ear and His heart. He wants to hear from His children. Jeremiah 33:3 (CSB) says, 'Call to me and I will answer you, and tell you great and incomprehensible things you do not know.' Philippians 4:6 is a call to 'not be anxious about anything, but in everything by prayer and supplication with thanksgiving let your requests be made known to God.' God desires His children to cry out to Him for themselves and for others. In 1 Thessalonians 5:17 we are commanded to 'pray without ceasing.' That means we need to be praying together and for others all the time.

Ephesians 6 describes warfare against cosmic powers of darkness and spiritual forces of evil we face as God's people. Paul exhorts the Ephesian church to be strong in the Lord and concludes with these words 6:18-19a, 'praying at all times in the Spirit, with all prayer and supplication. To that end, keep alert with all perseverance, making supplication for all the saints, and also for me...' Prayer for all the saints as well as for Paul himself, was imperative for their life together as they pushed back the attacks of their enemies in the spiritual realm. It's also our way of loving and serving one another spiritually as we face those same attacks and the spiritual opposition of this world.

---

34   Psalm 95:6-7, CSB

We should be praying together in our weekly corporate gathering, but there are various other ways we can carry out this command. Our church has a weekly midweek prayer group where all kinds of members, old and young alike, gather to intercede in prayer together for our church, community, and the world. We can also pray together in discipling relationships, small groups gatherings, coffee shops, parking lots or Bible study groups. We should be praying together, but also for one another. You can pray for members of your church by going through your church directory. Perhaps you may even find yourself praying in the middle of Walmart like I did a few months ago.

Covid had kept many of our older members from being able to gather corporately with us. In the sweet providence of God I ran into my dear friend, Tanner, in the middle of the frozen food section. He was masked and I was masked, but I knew it was him and was overjoyed to see him. His wife had been struggling with a number of health issues and when I asked how they were doing he began to cry. 'We miss gathering with the body so much.' Ugh. My heart was broken for my brother and I started to cry too. So what did we do? We stopped to pray together right there next to the frozen chicken nuggets and corn. I will never forget praying with my older brother and fellow partner for the gospel and feeling the joy that comes from sharing intercession to our Heavenly Father. (It even brought another shopper to tears to see us encourage one another in that way.) Sister, don't neglect the gift it is to obey God's command to pray with and for one another.

Longing for the eternal community with God

There's a scenario I find myself in often. A few things vary, but it stays remarkably consistent. I'm sitting across the table from a young lady who starts telling me her story of what it was like when she first came to our church. It usually goes something like this: 'I really wasn't sure what I thought about it the first time I visited.

I mean, in all honesty, I did not want to come back. All the lights were on, I could hear myself singing (and I don't like that at all!). The sermon was Bible focused. I liked that, but it was so much longer than I'm used to. And it was intense! I often had trouble concentrating in order to listen for that long. But when the service finished, I hung around for a while. So many people came over and introduced themselves to me and asked to get together. I'm not used to that. After a few weeks I looked forward to singing together and meeting back up with the people I'd met in previous weeks. I've made some new relationships and gotten together during the week with a number of them. The sermons are starting to make more sense. I think I'm beginning to understand this church community thing a little more.'

Christianity is a personal thing, but it isn't private. We don't go to church to see what we can get out of it and decipher afterwards how we feel, asking ourselves, 'Does this church meet my needs in this season of my life?' 'Are there people my age who I can do life with?' No! In fact it's quite the opposite. A local church is where we attach ourselves to a group of believers and make the commitment to see *them* built up in Christ. That is the picture God gives us of the New Testament church; many persons making up one body and all for the glory of God. There is a beautiful unity displayed in the diversity of our gathered body. And God spells out in His Word what our responsibilities of life together are. We are to strive to love one another, bearing with them and serving them, honoring them above ourselves. We are called to show hospitality and so spur one another along in the love and work God has called us to in Christ as we fellowship together. We are to submit to one another and the elders as unto the Lord and show regard for those who lead us and give us the Word of God in their teaching, all the while praying for one another and bringing our requests before God. These are no easy tasks, but because of God's love for us in Christ, we are freed to love others, for the love of Christ compels us.[35] Above all we are to 'put on love, which binds everything together in perfect harmony.'[36] This is a radical kind of community the world does not understand. It is the most important community of all time because it is a community that outlasts time. One day, my husband and I will no longer be able to swim, our kids will outgrow their soccer team, knitting will get old and the book club will end, but community built on Christ, committed to loving one another, will last for eternity. Our relationships will increase in joy as we see our Savior face-to-face and dwell with our God forevermore.

---

35   2 Corinthians 5:14

36   Colossians 3:14

QUESTIONS

'A DIFFERENT KIND OF COMMUNITY: LIFE WITH ONE ANOTHER'

Love is the foundation upon which we build our lives together in local churches. We carry one another's burdens and sorrows and rejoice with those who rejoice as we journey the road to heaven together. How we care for our church family matters to God.

1. How does love undergird all of our life together as a local church?

2. How does Jesus redefine family?

3. Do you find yourself fighting for connections with people in your local church? What steps can you take this week to develop relationships outside your normal sphere and comfort zone?

4. Do you have friendships in the church that make your non-Christian friends wonder why you spend time with them? If not, what steps can you make today to reach out to someone in your church who differs from you in some way?

5. Who might you be able to outdo in showing honor today?

6. If you have come from a home-life that was healthy and biblically centered, have you considered the importance of being that kind of family in the church to those who have never experienced a God honoring family life?

7. Do you inconvenience yourself for others?

8. How can you grow in your ability to submit to your leaders, making their job a joy and not a burden?

9. What is one way you can encourage an elder or the elders as a whole this next week?

10. List two things you can implement this week to grow in your prayer life for others.

Conclusion

A Heavenly Gathering

O Church of Christ upon that day,
When all are gathered in,
When every tear is wiped away
With every trace of sin;
Where justice, truth and beauty shine,
And death has passed away;
Where God and man will dwell as one,
For all eternity!

'O Church of Christ Invincible'
Matt Boswell

There is no perfect church. At least not right now. But that doesn't give us license to just love Jesus however we deem best. It also doesn't mean we give up and go rogue, doing the Christian life solo. There's no perfect church, but there are *healthy* churches. We should strive to find a healthy church, and give of ourselves wholeheartedly to the work of that church. Yet we do so never assuming it will be perfect or do things exactly the way we think best. Our goal is to do our part to help our church look more and more like the biblical model, while recognizing every church is filled with sinners, beginning with us! No one will get the church they want, but everyone will get the church they need.[1]

So ask questions like: Is the Word of God and the gospel boldly preached? Are the Scriptures the pattern for the church's gatherings and ministries? Is there biblical and godly leadership? Are people involved in each other's lives in meaningful and deliberate ways? Do I feel like this is a place I could grow and wouldn't be embarrassed to bring a non-Christian friend? The bathroom may need a remodel and the music may not exactly be your 'style,' but such things are incidental and not essential to growth in Christian maturity.

When it comes to your local church, invest yourself, however challenging it may seem. Get involved in the lives of others and open your life and home to them. 1 John 3:16 (CSB) tells us, 'This is how we have come to know love: He laid down his life for us. We should also lay down our lives for our brothers and sisters.' My dear sister, how can we obey this command if we have no brothers and sisters for whom we can lay down our lives? We need to be integrated into the family of our church so we can better display and proclaim the glory of God to a watching world.

The church is a new kind of community. A radical community. It is a community established by God Himself. We are a spiritual family brought together for the glory of God, to display that glory to the world. We are the body of Christ. We are His people, the sheep of His pasture! Come, let us truly worship and bow down before the Lord our maker, loving one another and demonstrating to the world the lavish love of God.

One day, very soon, this temporary family will become an eternal family. Then it will be a perfect community. *A community without sin*. A day is coming when all the shadows will be removed

---

1   Hanson, Collin and Leeman, Jonathan. *Rediscovering Church*, (Wheaton, IL: Crossway, 2021), p. 143.

and we will see clearly that which we have been longing for all our lives. We will see the face of Christ together. The wedding day with our bridegroom will commence. But not yet. Right now we are living in the dress rehearsal of that day. The anticipation is high, the people are gathering, but more must join us! Won't you invite them to the rehearsal to come and see, hear, and experience a little glimpse of what it will be like one day?

History starts and ends with a wedding. The in-between time is preparation for the end. Let us prepare for that day when we will gather in perfection at the table of the King, where the dwelling place of God is with man. For there He will dwell with us and we will be His people and God Himself will be our God. God gives us a glimpse of what it will be like in Revelation 21:1-5:

> Then I saw a new heaven and a new earth, for the first heaven and the first earth had passed away, and the sea was no more. And I saw the holy city, new Jerusalem, coming down out of heaven from God, prepared as a bride adorned for her husband. And I heard a loud voice from the throne saying, 'Behold, the **dwelling place of God is with man**.' He will dwell with them, and they will be his people, and God himself will be with them as their God. He will wipe away every tear from their eyes, and death shall be no more, neither shall there be mourning, nor crying, nor pain anymore, for the former things have passed away. And he who was seated on the throne said, 'Behold, I am making all things new' (emphasis mine).

What was only a shadow will one day become reality. We've only gotten a glimpse but one day our eyes will be opened wide. Let's celebrate that future reality by giving ourselves to the local church today! They are gatherings filled with glory. Will you join me as we wait patiently for that final day?

Acknowledgements

If you've spent any time with me at all you know how much I love to repeat the phrase, 'I'm just one beggar telling another beggar where to find bread.' Most fundamentally this book wouldn't have come about if the Lord had not set His mercy upon me and called me to Himself. I am honored to be chosen by Him. Fellow beggar, may you run to Him to find bread. Apart from Him you have no good thing! (Ps. 16:2). Thank you Lord Jesus for setting my heart free so I may run in the path of your commands. This book is a 'bouquet for thee.'[1]

Keri Folmar's continual encouragement and support every single step of the way is why you are holding this book in your hands. I've not met a woman who loves the Lord's Word and the Lord's people, especially His daughters, with as much passion as Keri. Keri lives what it looks like to choose the good portion (Luke 10:42). She's gifted, humble, and continually hoping in the promises of the Lord. (She was also very tenacious in her asking!) I am honored to have been included with the other writers in *The Good Portion* series. Thank you, Keri. I pray I grow to love Jesus and others with the passion you do, my dear sister and friend.

---

1   Elisabeth Elliott

God's providential plan brought my husband and me to Capitol Hill Baptist Church in May of 2000 and it was here that we had the privilege of knowing, loving, and ministering alongside Mark and Connie Dever. To know the Devers is to love and be loved by them. They opened their home and their hearts to us and each one of our children. We all grew to love God's bride, the church, because of their faithful ministry. (Mrs. Dever's house will always hold a special place in our kid's hearts). It was once said that more men came to faith through Edith Schaeffer's morning buns, than Francis Schaeffer's teaching, but I'd say, more people came to know God's love through the church because of Mark and Connie's ministry *together* for the church. Brad and I are eternally indebted to them for all the love and sacrifices they poured out on our behalf. Mark, how you ever had time to read my early draft I'll never know. Thank you big brother! I am humbled.

There were many people who prayed for, read through, asked about, encouraged, and supported me along the way. Katherine Brill, Chris Sutterfield, Scott Belinski, Ryan Troglin, and Sarah Highfill, and two of my own daughters, Page & Maggie, thank you for all your input and suggestions to make this book more accessible, readable, and enjoyable. Emalie Cockrell, you are a writing genius my friend. You were gracious and patient with the process (and hilarious). I love that God has put us together in this local church family.

A special thank you to my ministry sister, Leia Joseph. You're the best cheerleader a pastor's wife could have. Thank you for not only reading and engaging with the book in all its iterations, but praying and encouraging me along the way. What an adventure God has given us already, friend!

A special word of gratitude to the congregations that showed us a biblical picture of the family of God. Capitol Hill Baptist Church, Washington, D.C., Third Avenue Baptist Church, Louisville, KY, and University Baptist Church, Fayetteville, Arkansas, thank you! Warts and all, you loved us, cared for us, ministered to us, sharpened us, and helped us along this road to heaven as fellow sojourners. You have been, and UBC continues to be, the body of Christ to us. May God fortify and strengthen your witness to the world.

Our four children, Page, Maggie, William, and Elizabeth, a.k.a. my 'little friends,' have sacrificed and celebrated with me each step of the way. They showed incredible patience through the journey. I can't believe I get to be their mother. I'm so undeserving. I adore each one of you! In the words of the famous philosopher, Winnie the Pooh, 'Any day spent with you is my favorite day.' I pray you grow to love Christ's bride the church and live in fellowship with other believers.

To the one I love most in this world, my beloved husband, Brad. You make complementarity beautiful! More than anything, thank you for loving me as Christ loves the church. I love God more because of you and delight in knowing He chose me to be your partner on our journey heavenward. You know what this project took and you walked with me through every single step of it. Your editing, your conversations, your prayers, your encouragement through my tears, you carried me through to the end. Thank you! This was my half court shot and I stood on your shoulders, brother.

Selected Bibliography

Theologies

Berkof, Louis. *Systematic Theology.* (Edinburgh, UK: The Banner of Truth Trust, 2000).

Bray, Gerald. *God is Love: A Biblical and Systematic Theology.* (Wheaton, IL: Crossway, 2012).

Culver, Robert Duncan. *Systematic Theology: Biblical & Historical.* (Ross-Shire, UK: Christian Focus Publications, 2005).

Grudem, Wayne. *Systematic Theology: An Introduction to Biblical Doctrine.* (Leicester, UK: IVP and Grand Rapids, Michigan: Zondervan, 1994).

Horton, Michael. *The Christian Faith: A Systematic Theology for Pilgrims On the Way.* (Grand Rapids, MI: Zondervan, 2011).

Books

Anyabwile, Thabiti. *Finding Faithful Elders & Deacons.* (Wheaton, IL: Crossway, 2012).

Bonhoeffer, Dietrich. *Life Together.* (New York, NY: Harper & Row, 1954).

Butterfield, Rosaria. *The Gospel Comes with a House Key: Practicing Radically Ordinary Hospitality in Our Post-Christian World.* (Wheaton, IL: Crossway, 2018).

Calvin, John. *A Little Book on the Christian Life.* Ann Arbor, MI: Reformation Trust Publishing, 2017)

Clowney, Edmund P. *The Church.* (Downers Grove, IL: IVP, 1995).

Dever, Mark. *Building Healthy Churches Series: Discipling: How to Help Others Follow Jesus.* (Wheaton, IL: Crossway, 2016).

Dever, Mark. *The Church.* (Nashville, TN: B&H Publishing, 2012).

Dever, Mark. *Understanding Church Leadership.* (Nashville, TN: B&H Publishing, 2016).

Dever, Mark. *Why Should I Join a Church?* (Wheaton, IL: Crossway, 2020).

Dever, Mark. *Nine Marks of a Healthy Church.* (Wheaton, IL: Crossway, 2004).

Dever, Mark and Dunlop, Jamie. *The Compelling Community: Where God's Power Makes a Church Attractive.* (Wheaton, IL: Crossway, 2015).

Dever, Mark and Leeman, Jonathan. *Baptist Foundations.* (Nashville, RN: B&H Publishing, 2015).

DeYoung, Kevin and Gilbert, Greg. *What is the Mission of the Church? Making Sense of Social Justice, Shalom, and the Great Commission.* (Wheaton, IL: Crossway, 2011).

Green, Christopher. *The Message of the Church.* (Nottingham, UK: IVP. 2013).

Hanson, Collin and Leeman, Jonathan. *Rediscovering Church.* (Wheaton, IL: Crossway, 2021).

Hill, Megan. *A Place to Belong: Learning to Love the Local Church.* (Wheaton, IL: Crossway, 2020).

Hill, Megan. *Praying Together: The Priority & Privilege of Prayer in Our Homes, Communities, and Churches.* (Wheaton, IL: Crossway, 2019).

James, Sharon. *God's Design for Women in an Age of Gender Confusion.* (Evangelical Press, 2019)

Jamieson, Bobby. *Going Public: Why Baptism is Required for Church Membership.* (Nashville, TN: B&H Publishing, 2015).

Jamieson, Bobby. *Understanding Baptism,* (Nashville, RN: B&H Publishing, 2016).

Jamieson, Bobby. *Understanding the Lord's Supper,* (Nashville, RN: B&H Publishing, 2016).

Lawrence, Michael. *Biblical Theology in the Life of the Church: A Guide for Ministry.* (Wheaton, IL: Crossway, 2010).

Leeman, Jonathan. *Building Healthy Churches Series: Church Discipline: How the Church Protects the Name of Jesus.* (Wheaton, IL: Crossway, 2016).

Leeman, Jonathan. *Don't Fire your Church Members: A Case for Congregationalism.* (Nashville, TN: B&H Publishing, 2016).

Leeman, Jonathan. *Reverberation: How God's Word Brings Light, Freedom, and Action to His People.* (Chicago, IL: Moody Publishers, 2011).

Leeman, Jonathan. *The Rule of Love: How the Local Church Should Reflect God's Love & Authority.* (Wheaton, IL: Crossway, 2018).

Leeman, Jonathan. *Understanding Church Discipline.* (Nashville, TN: B&H Publishing, 2016).

Leeman, Jonathan. *Understanding the Congregation's Authority.* (Nashville, TN: B&H Publishing, 2016)

Lister, Ryan. *Emblems of the Infinite King.* (Wheaton, IL: Crossway, 2019).

Lloyd-Jones, Dr. Martin. *God's Ultimate Purpose: An Exposition of Ephesians 1.* (Grand Rapids, MI: Baker Books, 1979).

Lloyd-Jones, Dr. Martin. *God's Way of Reconciliation: An Exposition of Ephesians 2.* (Grand Rapids, MI: Baker Books, 1972).

Lloyd-Jones, Dr. Martin. *The Unsearchable Riches of Christ: An Exposition of Ephesians 3.* (Grand Rapids, MI: Baker Books, 1979).

Lloyd-Jones, Dr. Martin. *Christian Unity: An Exposition of Ephesians 4:1-6.* (Grand Rapids, MI: Baker Books, 1981).

Rinne, Jeramie. *Building Healthy Churches Series: Church Elders: How to Shepherd God's People Like Jesus.* (Wheaton, IL: Crossway, 2016).

Menikoff, Aaron. *Character Matters: Shepherding in the Fruit of the Spirit.* (Chicago, IL: Moody Publishers, 2020).

Schreiner, Thomas R. and Crawford, Matthew R. *The Lord's Supper: Remembering & Proclaiming Christ Until He Comes.* (Nashville, TN: B&H Publishing, 2010).

Smethurst, Matt. *Building Healthy Churches Series: Deacons: How they Serve & Strengthen the Church.* (Wheaton, IL: Crossway, 2021).

Smith, Claire. *God's Good Design: What the Bible Really Says about Men & Women.* (Matthias Media; 2nd edition, 2019)

Wellum, Stephen, *Baptism and the Relationship between the Covenants* in *Believer's Baptism,* ed. by Schreiner and Wright, (Nashville, TN: B&H Academic, 2006).

Wilkin, Jen. *Women of the Word.* (Wheaton, IL: Crossway, 2014).

Articles

TGC Article. Carter, Paul

https://ca.thegospelcoalition.org/columns/ad-fontes/should-pastors-be-paid/

IX Marks article. Jamieson, Bobby.

https://www.9marks.org/article/how-the-lords-supper-makes-a-local-church/

IX Marks article. Wheeler, Erin. https://www.9marks.org/article/the-sweet-rewards-of-a-quiet-ministry/

Scripture Index

Christian Focus Publications

Our mission statement –

STAYING FAITHFUL

In dependence upon God we seek to impact the world through literature faithful to His infallible Word, the Bible. Our aim is to ensure that the Lord Jesus Christ is presented as the only hope to obtain forgiveness of sin, live a useful life and look forward to heaven with Him.

Our Books are published in four imprints:

CHRISTIAN FOCUS

popular works including biographies, commentaries, basic doctrine and Christian living.

CHRISTIAN HERITAGE

books representing some of the best material from the rich heritage of the church.

MENTOR

books written at a level suitable for Bible College and seminary students, pastors, and other serious readers. The imprint includes commentaries, doctrinal studies, examination of current issues and church history.

CF4•K

children's books for quality Bible teaching and for all age groups: Sunday school curriculum, puzzle and activity books; personal and family devotional titles, biographies and inspirational stories – Because you are never too young to know Jesus!

Christian Focus Publications Ltd,
Geanies House, Fearn, Ross-shire,
IV20 1TW, Scotland, United Kingdom.
www.christianfocus.com